AF505754

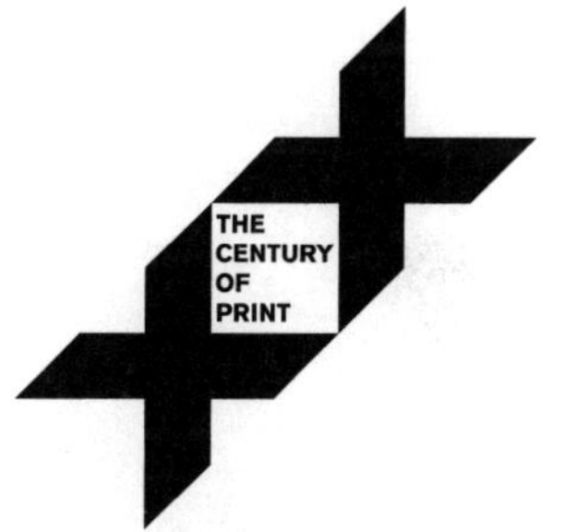
THE
CENTURY
OF
PRINT

BAUHAUSBÜCHER

13

EDITORS:
WALTER GROPIUS
L. MOHOLY-NAGY

ALBERT GLEIZES
CUBISM

ALBERT GLEIZES
CUBISM

LARS MÜLLER PUBLISHERS

Translation by JANE MICHAEL

BY THE SAME AUTHOR:

DU CUBISME
with the collaboration of Jean Metzinger
Figuière publisher 1912

CUBISME
Geneva 1918

DU CUBISME ET DES MOYENS DE LE COMPRENDRE
J. Povolozky 1920

LA MISSION CRÉATRICE DE L'HOMME DANS LE DOMAINE PLASTIQUE
J. Povolozky 1922

LA PEINTURE ET SES LOIS
"What should result from Cubism"
Paris 1924

VERS UNE CONSCIENCE PLASTIQUE
Articles and lectures 1911—25
J. Povolozky 1926

LA MACHINE MODERNOLATRIE
In preparation

PEINTURE ET PERRSPECTIVE DESCRIPTIVE
Moly-Sabata publisher, Sablons, Isère

Originally published in German
under the title of "Kubismus" by
Albert Langen Verlag München
in 1928; printed by Hesse & Becker
Leipzig; printing blocks by
C. Dünnhaupt & Co. Dessau.
First English edition published by
Lars Müller, based on the first German
edition, translated from French
to German by Eulein Grohmann.

ISBN 978-3-03778-666-6
Printed in Germany
www.lars-mueller-publishers.com

TYPOGRAPHY, COVER, JACKET: L. MOHOLY-NAGY
REPRODUCTION: INTEGRAL LARS MÜLLER
PRINTING: DZA DRUCKEREI ZU ALTENBURG
PRINTED IN GERMANY

CONTENTS

I.
THE HISTORY OF CUBISM

The works of Cubism came as a great surprise because nobody was sufficient=
ly well prepared for a movement that they were able to predict what would be
coming on the basis of what already existed.
For some time doubts had been expressed regarding the idea of form which
had been adopted from the Renaissance. During the course of the nineteenth
century, scholarship and the initiative of a group of academics had rediscov=
ered Christian art. To confront the generally recognized Latin absolutism with
such a powerful and qualified opponent meant the challenge of a discussion at
least; and furthermore, it also meant the possibility of a concept of form which
contradicted that which had been preached by the authority of Latinism.
The consequences of this fact could be felt immediately in the practical sphere
of the arts. The Romanticism of a Delacroix, the Realism of a Courbet, and
Impressionism, which sacrificed everything to the impression of the senses,
could all be traced back to the historical concept of the independence and
greatness of Christian composition. These artists challenged the Académie
to a contest by confronting the rigid expression preached by the latter with
an expression of emotion; by preferring the lively dynamism of a developing
form over rigid volume in space. Within their sphere they destroyed the cir=
cumstances of the official art scene, but were doubtless still unaware that in
order to achieve a restructuring it would have required means other than those
at their disposal. And so their role was simply to shake the main pillars of
the ancient building, but without being able to demolish it. Human memory
is faced with a difficult task when confronted with intellectual change.
Schooled by Impressionism and the Realism of a Manet, Cézanne was able
to use a number of earlier experiences to his advantage. This explains the
bold and curious structure of his oeuvre, that hybrid being, in which the rigid,

descriptive concept of form dating from the Renaissance seeks to achieve unity with the desire for a flexible, concrete idea of form and to assert itself, whereby the form increasingly prevailed. The fundamental contradictions of this oeuvre are ultimately the reason for its popularity; everyone can find in it what he needs at that time. To date, no one has been able or willing to recognize that Cézanne is no closer to the Renaissance than what we understand under the term Romanticism. His approach is that of a hesitant person who is torn between tradition and new experiments, which however are never conclusive. His generation saw in him only powerless desire, because they were too close to him. The following generations, on the other hand, which lacked a coherent context themselves, and who were torn on the one hand between a powerless mental state and that diffuse striving for intellectual renewal on the other, raised the master artist from Aix to the summit of fame, precisely because of his hesitation. The crassest contradictions disappeared before the infallibility of this deity. Cézanne was worshiped as a god both by the Classicists, who saw in him the descriptive and the perspectival, and also the revolutionaries, because they recognized in him a constructive will, a revolt against the descriptive, admittedly a timid one, but nonetheless an undeniable attempt to reconstruct the geometric plane on the vertical one, in other words virtually a rejection of perspective. What is certain is that the Cubists could not miss these attempts made by Cézanne; and so, like so many others, they approved of his works, albeit on the basis of their own very specific preconditions.

We must position the artists' group known as the Fauves — Matisse, Derain and Friesz — between Cézanne and the Cubists. They were influenced not only by Cézanne, but also by Van Gogh and Gauguin, who were by no means as far removed from the proclamation of the new idea as people have later attempted to claim. I have emphasized on a number of occasions that for various reasons, men like Sérusier, Maurice Denis, Seurat, Cross, Signac, and Odilon Redon were pioneers of the order which was just developing, without realizing it themselves. We cannot be so naive in all earnest as to assume that a single individual is sufficient to bring about a radical change that was so difficult and so complex as the one required by the current status of painting. Such an opinion would contradict the entire experience of history, because each transformation can be traced back to the sum of a number of significant efforts which took effect simultaneously and successively. By no means does it require those unconscious, enthusiastic fashion geniuses to achieve such a transformation; instead, intelligent, talented men are needed, who sacrifice the transitory interests of personal vanity to a distant, altruistic goal.

Convinced of the significance of Cubism for mankind, I have always endeav⸗ ored to determine its true origin out of a conscious or unconscious partnership of a group of people, but I know very well that the last word has not yet been spoken here. It will take a long time and the endeavors of future generations until these first traces of the discovery can become a wide path which can be trodden by everyone.

The pronounced interest of our time in archaeology continued the work of emancipation begun by the Romantic scholars and helped in its turn to reject the exclusive claims of the Renaissance dogma. Officially, it sufficed to describe certain periods of history as elementary, primitive, and tentative, without however bestowing on them an exemplary power. The reason for this was not only the view that people had of the Renaissance, but rather the belief in con⸗ tinuous progress. Historical Materialism believed that it was possible to dis⸗ entangle the secrets of the origin starting from the Prehistoric Era, the com⸗ placent hubris that confuses civilization with the introduction of machines, those tools of progress which work towards the dissemination of inferior and demoralizing products. To this day, you can still come across the reproach that this or that artist is influenced by archaic ideas, and on the other hand, there is also a recognition for unimportant poor imitations of so⸗called periods of civilization. The independent artists judged these things differently.
In their boldness, they were able to go further than their predecessors in the nineteenth century, who admired the character of Pre⸗Renaissance Christian forms, a synthesis of the southern and the Nordic characteristics on a Celtic foundation. They could have recourse to incomparable riches in the history of mankind, which the historical material of the time offered them. Starting from the Christian Era, they could thus discover new countries and be inspired by their artworks, which they found to be just as beautiful as those from their own past. They exploited these discoveries, which were unknown to most of their contemporaries, and thus with little effort became famous as original innovators. Fashion took advantage of the opportunity, because it saw the change of renewal in these newly discovered sources. What have we not seen

in the public exhibitions of these last twenty=five years by way of pictures in the style of the Egyptians, Hindus, Chinese, Indians, Negroes! These appear= ances may have lacked depth but they were not without result: they, too, helped with the establishment of a new frame of mind; it will take the place of the time that will die with us, in order to introduce a new era according to the rhythmic law of life.

The beginnings of Cubism stood under the influence of Archaism and Primi= tivism. It saw its origins not so much in the Greek precepts of the Age of Pericles or the High Renaissance, but rather in those works that civilization was ashamed of. Because it studied them and loved them, it could dare to express itself in forms that were generally declared to be madness, and yet they were based in part on old Roman paintings and in part on Negro sculp= ture and a profound humanity. This change in historical relationships formed the starting point for all new experiments. Together with the Cubists, others were also enthralled by these eras that had been decried by the Academies, because it is precisely this enthusiasm which characterizes our present genera= tion. It is perhaps unfair towards the Romantics at times, but it cannot ignore the fact that it was above all to them that it owed that other inspiration which the official teaching, saturated with the catchphrases of the Renaissance, could not pass on to them. So, in short, here lie the preconditions for Cubism. Initially it still goes along with the other directions of its generation, but the time seems to be near when it will assume the leadership; when it will assert itself over the external appearances; when it will transform the still=present intellectual admiration for those past eras into an artistic knowledge of eter= nal laws. It will influence not only the painters, the sculptors, and the architects, but the whole of our age.

In 1911, on the occasion of the exhibition of the "Indépendants" in Paris, the public found itself looking for the first time at a collection of paintings that were not branded. That may contradict the accounts that are in circulation, but it is the truth.

I have before me a short excerpt from the evening newspaper "La Presse" about the Salon d'automne of 1910, which aptly describes the attitude to the new, scarcely comprehensible painterly experiments: "The geometric follies

of a Metzinger, Le Fauconnier and Gleizes." It hardly presages
friendly comments in future! Braque and Picasso exhibited only in the
Galerie Kahnweiler, where we ignored them. Robert Delaunay, Metzinger,
and Le Fauconnier came to our attention immediately on the occasion of
the Salon des Indépendants in 1910, although no slogan was applied to them.
Consequently it is clear that the term "Cubism" was not in circulation at
that time, however much people may try to maintain the contrary.
In 1911 the events were precipitated, resulting in clarity about the significance
and nature of the crisis in painting that was just beginning. Room 41 at the
"Indépendants" was a revelation for everyone. Nobody could remain un-
touched by its powerful effect. It roused tempers like a natural phenomenon
that does not have to be understood in order to shock people and make
them afraid when it erupts. Did these canvases painted in gray-in-gray not
herald a future in which today's forms were destroyed and replaced by others?
In the face of these newcomers, people felt they must plead for the legitimacy
of the great Renaissance masters*), who are nonetheless uncontested in their
omnipotence. The minds which could not distinguish between the contemporary and the eternal cannot decide to recognize in particular the fundamental characteristic of all being in change.
Initially, the painters who were responsible were the ones who were most surprised at this uproar which they had unleashed, involuntarily, simply because
they had hung on the boarding of the barracks building on the Cours-La-Reine
the paintings that they had created with such care, conviction, and also with
inner excitement.
It was from this season that the term Cubism originated.
Never before had a crowd of onlookers that was so passionately excited been
seen in front of concepts and especially works of fine art, silent paintings.
Never was the criticism as violent as during that period. I shall record the names
of the artists who were the cause of this frenzy without wanting to be: Jean
Metzinger, Le Fauconnier, Fernand Léger, Robert Delaunay, and myself. Out
of all this, it is illuminating to note that these paintings seemed to represent
a threat to the order whose unshakeability people had hitherto believed in.
In almost all the newspaper reports, people lost their heads; they started to say
that "it was unnecessary to broadcast opinions about the Cubists, who were

---

*) Georges Mourey, "Salon d'Automne," Le Journal, 1911.

of no importance," and then they angrily dedicated to them seven of the ten columns allotted to the essay about the Salon at the time. You could write some very interesting studies about the press in general if you were to take the time to work through the reports in the daily papers and magazines of that period. Nor was Cubism the attraction of a single season or a larger or smaller interest group. There was nothing artificial about the furore that it aroused because it had not developed from careful consideration; it was not staged by artists in search of fame and publicity who had sought attention, and provoked it by appeals to the public. The pictures of the time prove this all too clearly. Compared with the present-day achievements of Cubism or with many different types of painting that have appeared since then, which primarily sought loud success, those pictures are astonishingly dignified and simple.

In the Salon d'automne of 1911, the outbursts of anger erupted again, with the same violence as in the case of the "Indépendants." I can still remember Room 8 of the Grand Palais on opening day. People crowded in, laughed, shouted, intended to give us a bad time. And which pictures had we hung there? Metzinger showed his fine canvas "Tea Time," Léger his earnest "Nudes in a Landscape," Le Fauconnier, "Landscapes from Savoie," and I exhibited "The Hunt" and the "Portrait of Jacques Nayral." How long ago it all was! And yet I can still see the crowd which was jammed in the doorways of the room, pushing aside the densely packed visitors who wanted to get in to see the monsters that we were at close quarters.

The Paris winter season used this event to add spice to its distractions. While the newspapers blew the call to arms in order to warn of the danger and to summon the help of the public authorities, to the delight of all blockheads, the cabarettists, the presenters of revues and other buffoons indulged in ambiguities about the "Cube." They discovered that this word was suitable like no other to arouse laughter, and that is, as everyone knows, the fundamental characteristic of the human race.

It was inevitable that the more people loudly attempted to stop the spread of the troublesome idea, the more the movement gained ground. It quickly passed beyond the borders of its country of origin. The whole world was involved with Cubism. The invitations to exhibitions increased because people wanted to get to know it. Many arrived from Germany, from Russia, from Belgium, Switzerland, Holland, Austria-Hungary, Bohemia. The artists took up some of them, and writers like Guillaume Apollinaire, Maurice

Raynal, André Salmon, Alexandre Mercereau, and the Chief Prosecutor Granié supported them with their pens and with their words.

In the other countries of Europe, the scandal did not provoke the same furore as in Paris, but people were equally interested in Cubism, and public opinion became excited about these new prospects in painting. What reached us in those times was an echo of the opinions expressed by the European public through a trusting or malicious press. They told the most fantastic stories, published portraits and reproductions, mostly retouched unilaterally if not entirely invented, and proved how easy it is for the imagination to tear large numbers of individuals out of their dull ordinariness if you simply electrify them with some sort of lively spark. It seemed amazing in the past that thousands of people in Greece could be enthralled by a work by Sophocles. Cubism showed that this passion still exists today, if you think back to the boundless discussions for which it served as the starting point, and which are by no means over even today, after eighteen years of lively development.

At the Salon d'automne of 1911, a number of new talents had gathered round the men of that first hour: André Lhote, Marcel Duchamp, Roger de La Fresnaye, and Jacques Villon. And then on the other hand, Juan Gris, although he did not exhibit with us: that persistent investigator, who would subsequently be one of the first to recognize the fundamental elements of Cubism, which at that time was still permeated by traditional moments which people clung to determinedly. None of us wanted to become reconciled to the scandal, which still persisted. We were all without a personal fortune, and it became even harder for us when we saw in it the reason why buyers continued to avoid us. They had not dared to purchase works at that time with impunity for which there was no guarantee of economic success.

People will believe without hesitation that I say this not out of personal interest, but what tremendous, altruistic courage reigned in those heroic days among my fellow comrades-in-arms! I cannot think of those moments without admiring the natural magnanimity of their actions. And the significance of this behavior should not be underestimated. These painters, who could be seen at the "Indépendants" and at the Salon d'automne of 1911, deserve without doubt the glory of having planted in the human race of that time a seed which through its natural development would burst the concept of form that was current in those days.

The attacks of public authority instigated by the main press organs of Paris and on the insistence of the Académie were directed towards these artists, and these artists alone. The municipal council of Paris threatened the Salon des "Indépendants," from which Cubism had emerged, with excommunication. Interpellations against the Cubist painters were presented in the Chamber of Deputies. Marcel Sembat raised his voice in order to support them and at the same time to support the Salon d'automne, whose most important leading members lost their heads. "This year (1912), the Salon d'automne has had the honor of being the subject of a scandal, and it owes this scandal to the Cubist painters." Sembat began his speech with these words, and the speech was an important event in the history of our times. For the first time, an ethical, ideational, intellectual question was raised in a parliament. For the first time, the legitimate existence and the superiority of an unofficial artistic opinion was pronounced in public. What had hitherto been said in small gatherings, now rang out loud and clear from the heights of a national rostrum. And from both camps, interjections were heard which indicated agreement. Painting called on literature for help; Cubism reawakened the memory of Mallarmé, and the Symbolist poets became modern again.

If such an event had happened in Greece or Rome, our ossified humanists would have not been able to resist expressing their recognition and admiration. But in such close proximity to us it did not seem worthy of further notice. Nonetheless, we may be allowed to prophesy that it will become important when the new spirit which is rising searches for heroes in the present day; when it has come to power and ascertains who its predecessors in an earlier era were. Incidentally, the paintings which prompted the scandal and the courageous defense will be there, and these witnesses will provide even better proof that something new was in the making. History has already decided about the actual foundation of this period by not allowing anything to survive which was not really strong and resilient, and it will therefore ensure that justice will be done to each one of them according to the measure of his works. Then people will recognize that here indeed are the great works of an era that was otherwise in decline; only the uncertainty and the errors of calculation have contributed to the fact that these documents were ignored in silence.

So that the memory may survive, I note that at the "Indépendants" of 1912, Metzinger showed "Woman with Horse," Léger a "Group of People," Le Fauconnier a sketch for the "Hunter," Delaunay his vast "City of Paris," and

I showed "The Bathers"; in the Salon d'automne of the same year, Metzinger exhibited "Dancer in a Café," Léger "Woman in Blue," Le Fauconnier the "Hunter," and I "Man on a Balcony." The "Section d'Or" exhibition was also held in Paris in the winter of 1912; this was the most important private event at that time and assembled the best talents of the generation, all of whom agreed to show their works under the banner of Cubism. At the same time, Jean Metzinger and I published the first written work about Cubism, "Du 'Cubisme'," which was published by Figuière Paris. We wanted to attempt to introduce a little order into the chaos of everything that had been published in newspapers and magazines since 1911. Shortly afterwards, Guillaume Apol=linaire published a study on the new painting, in which goodwill and poetic talent took the place of the actual treatment of the question. It was also pub=lished by Figuière with the title "Les Peintres Cubistes, Méditations Esthétiques." The year 1913 saw the further development of the movement. The changes it had undergone since the "Indépendants" of 1911 permitted no further doubts about its nature. Cubism was not a school characterized by a superficial feature; it was the radical new order of a state of mind that was developing. Each year showed it in a new stage, caught up in continuous growth like a living body. Its enemies might perhaps have forgiven it if it had come and gone like a fashion; but their bitterness grew when they realized that it would survive beyond the lifetimes of the painters who were responsible for its beginnings. In the "Salon des Indépendants" of 1913 we saw a major work by Jean Metzinger, "The Blue Bird"; "The Cardiff Team" by Robert Delaunay; two important paintings by Léger; a still life and the "Man in a Café" by Juan Gris; works full of enthusiasm by La Fresnaye, Marcoussis, and others; and by me, at last, "The Football Players."

For the Salon d'automne of 1913, which in general was presented under the banner of Cubism, Metzinger had sent his large painting "The Boat," La Fresnaye "The Conquest of the Air," and I sent "The Fishing Boats" and "Town and River." The interest in Cubism continued unabated, although the first surprise was over; anger and enthusiasm had not changed their sides in the fight; the opponents retained their positions. To be convinced of this you need only to read the pamphlets by Louis Vauxcelles in Gil Blas from 1913, alongside the eulogies by Guillaume Apollinaire in L'Intransigeant.

In order to complete the prewar period, I now need only recall the last Salon des Indépendants in 1914, where once again we also exhibited important paintings, including the "Simultaneous Circles" by Robert Delaunay, which I shall speak of again shortly.

What has happened to all the works I have listed above? Most of them are in German museums and collections. The rest are scattered: some are in France, others in America, Russia, Spain ..., current events have not allowed us to trace their fates. Since they normally seldom appear in public auctions due to the art market which dominates the world, they are either forgotten or unknown. How interesting it would be to bring them together one day and show them publicly once more! After the passage of so many years, it would be possible to understand the history of contemporary art better through these works, because they would shift the hangers-on who distort the picture today into the place that they deserve.

Thus between 1911 and 1914, Cubism developed from the concept "body" (volume) to the concept "mobility" (cinématique), which finally destroyed the perspectival unity of the Renaissance.
Robert Delaunay even had the intuition of a synthetic form, which took the place of the concept of the static fragmentary form, as it is depicted in the perspectival unity or in the multiplicity of points of view. Evidently it remained in the space; it remained all too visual, there is no doubt of that; it was too powerfully dominated by the interplay of sensuous impressions. Nonetheless, he had the intimation of a new one; he brushed past it; he announced it loudly in the picture that he called Simultaneous Circles. And today it moves me deeply, because I have every reason to believe that I now understand what was not clear to me at the time. When I say this, it is possible that many people are surprised because they think of the Robert Delaunay of today, who has returned to descriptive paintings. I cannot help them if they refuse to see that in 1913 Delaunay announced the aim of Cubism. I for my part admit that the deeper I explore the problem of form as it was categorically postulated by Cubism in 1911, the more Delaunay's work from 1913 gains in importance. And so, in conclusion, I admit quite frankly that at the time he was the only one of all of us who conceived the ideas most clearly and correctly and in a unique manner, through his outstanding talent and supported by an effervescent and healthy vigor.

Behind these sumptuous colors, under this motif of monotonous circles, beyond all the gimmicky modernism, we sense the proximity of heaven; we knew what Mallarmé called the "azure": the perception of the compositional in time, perfect, final, circling, astronomical. Delaunay played with moons and suns like a marveling child. I am delighted today to know that this possibly unintentional work lies behind us, which nonetheless was so full of promise because it was full of spontaneous and bold ideas.

Delaunay's contribution to this age was realizable by no one else except for himself. He could anticipate many things because he had no reason to be cautious. The window that he had broken after a wide expanse of light was the proof of an unprecedented boldness: the descriptive element of formal analysis was immediately dissolved in it and a new form began to circle there obliviously, a form which was still unknown to us, which we could not yet adopt; the motionless had been transformed into motion.

We clung so tightly to the descriptive picture; we dissected the form, its aspects, the perspective; we turned the object this way and that in our hands; we turned around it; we anxiously followed this mystery of form. Delaunay did not know worries of this kind; he saw the object as "something that moves in a circle." We could not join him with a compositional manner created in this way, especially as this composition did not emerge from the atmosphere which it even emphasized. But I repeat: he saw a truly new compositional state at a single glance; or better still: he proclaimed the return of a composition which had only been valid at certain times and with a completely different mentality from ours, which none of us had abandoned as yet. And without such abandonment there can be no new beginning; the most unheard-of intuitions remain without consequence, and the most careful analysis without result.

To summarize: The following facts seem to me to be irrefutable from the prewar years:

On the one hand the work of a Braque and Picasso, with whom we must also include Juan Gris, who live and work independently, who have already been captured by the art dealers, who have moved on past the analysis of volume and of the object, and who are approaching the real substance of painting, the compositional nature (nature plastique) of the flat surface.

And on the other, in the breach, in the thick of the battle which is just beginning, Jean Metzinger, Le Fauconnier, Fernand Léger, and myself; we are occupied mentally with investigations of gravity, density, volume, the analysis of the object; we study the dynamics of the lines; we finally embrace the surface in its true being.

And finally, Robert Delaunay; he overflows, he is insufficiently master of himself to linger over analytical investigations, but his intuition regarding the aim of Cubism is completely clear.

●

Sadly, the artists were dispersed between 1914 and 1918; nonetheless a reflection and consolidation of this new state of mind, which opposes the one which still prevails today and without which a fundamental transformation cannot be realized, could only be advantageous. On the other hand, Cubism achieved a significant consolidation in the development of its technical resources. The surface or plane became the obvious starting point for all painting. The word composition, which until then had been regarded exclusively as an important part of the bodies within space, gained a meaning that corresponded more truly to the senses, whether they were real as in sculpture and architecture, or an optical illusion as in drawing and painting. This was a result of the fact that the composition no longer remained the subject of an intellectual consideration, but became at last a consideration of the sensuous means of representation, by means of which the form changed their dimensions as they changed their direction. The insight that sculpture had lost because it believed itself to be dependent upon the description and the perspective that determined it, reappeared, thanks to the simple recognition of the representational material with which the painter was dealing: the flat surface of the wall. Painters like Jean Metzinger and Juan Gris who were intent upon providing rigorous general rules in accordance with the truth in the confusing experiments, can primarily take the credit for having worked on the determination of the elements. As painters who had stood at the beginning of the movement, they were the first and the best placed to determine the fundamentals of the new order which was in the process of emerging.

I have often stated my opinion about these two men quite openly. The importance of artists like Gris goes far beyond the apparent bleakness of his painting, which can be explained by the mere fact that he never wanted to use skillful tricks to hide what he did not know. He said everything that he did know with utter clarity, and his work is a treasure chest of lessons for young artists who, in their respect for the craft that they have chosen, do not appre⸗ ciate that painting is at the mercy of irresponsibility, which is known as genius and which is basically nothing other than incurable laziness. Gris supplies an example of the greatest technical conscientiousness that I know of; and he shows that painting only grants her gifts to those who come to her after they have sworn to wait patiently. Gris did not possess the lightness of the virtuoso; he always discovered difficulties when he composed his paint⸗ ing; he was not a brilliant colorist; he was not skilled in the fine interplay of the nuances of color. But what a wise and shrewd mind!

Jean Metzinger, whose clear intellect I learned to value when we wrote "Du 'Cubism'" together, developed the indispensable basis for the true technique of painting with infinite knowledge and admirable thoroughness in turn and at the same time as Gris. While the others continued their experiments practically with greater or lesser success, depending on their talent and for⸗ tune — and I beg you to believe that I count myself among them — Metzinger discovered with the clarity of a physicist the basic reasons for construction, without the basis of which no progress is possible. I say this completely without prejudice and make no allowances for the commonly regarded tra⸗ dition, which was spread by certain interested parties and which then expand⸗ ed as a result of those thousand random factors which such opinions bring into being. My aim is to relate the true history of Cubism, whose starting point was not a game of chance but which was firmly anchored in the general reassessment whose imperative necessity stands today beyond all doubt.

●

For this reason, I consider it necessary to say a few words about the tenden⸗ tious machinations which led to the fact that a false version has been put in the place of the true history of Cubism. It primarily benefits the old mental state which is in the process of disappearing and which makes us believe in its continued existence.

During the difficult years from 1914 until 1919, when its supporters were scattered and concerned about the future, Cubism, which had fallen into disrepute as a result of the usual forms of patriotic slander, was not able to escape from the tempting goodwill of snobbery. Perhaps it believed that it

would secure its existence if it took shelter here. In the case of a small number of representatives, Cubism became dependent upon the artificial society of sophisticated circles, where money increasingly provided the sole accolade. Thus it appeared to have achieved its goal when otherwise, degraded to a private hobby, it would have had no further aim but to carve out a career.
I do not want to dwell at length here on the legends of these individual cases, but want only to direct the interest which has declined today towards these facts, with the aim of making what follows comprehensible.
Understandably, this biased attitude of snobbery towards what it did not understand in Cubism, which incidentally vanished just as quickly as it had appeared, aroused the activity of commercial passions. Cubism aroused the hopes of wealth, just as the manufacture of cannon and poison gas had done. But it did not find customers quite as easily. The muddled nature of snobbery very quickly disappointed dealers, after they had filled it with hope only a short while previously: the Cubist products did not sell well. There was no return on the money they had spent. No clientèle was formed, apart from a few nouveaux riches who were taken in and numbers of professional collectors. The stocks increased and remained in the cellars and labyrinthine shops. The international organization of the art trade revolted against the continuation of the adventure. It assumed the task of giving Cubism a meaning that corresponded to their present and future interests. They narrowed it down as they thought best. They interpreted it, prescribed the direction in which it should progress, forced it to gradually return to all that which it had revolted against since its first appearance. The snobbery, which a few years previously had occurred only in the case of the worst academic concoctions, and which had accepted Cubism purely by chance, returned to its true taste with the convenient gesture of forgiveness. The moment was no longer far away in which Academicism in modern guise, that is to say, basically skillfully sabotaged, could be offered to it with the prospect of success.

The postwar era made all this manifest itself even more starkly. The difficulties with which the art sector had to cope; the growing authority of the dealers of all kinds, who gained access to the highest positions in the social hierarchy; the discredit which it became increasingly difficult to deny, in which the intangible values which could not be quantified in numbers declined; the uncertainty of all the facts of life, which exhausted all patience — all these causes and many others gave rise to the predominant improbable state under which we all suffer, without summoning up the real courage to protest. As during the war, speculators personally occupied the seats of ministers in order to be able to better follow the progress of their business, instead of remaining behind the scenes and pulling the strings of the political marionettes, who keep the exploitation of the people within certain boundaries of decency. Thus, the same procedure took place after the war in the sphere of art.

When will they finally take a stand against the interests which supposedly serve the development of art, but which are obviously focused too much on business? As the need arises, they give events a turn in such a way that an uncritical public is inclined to take them at face value. Their effect on the unrest of young artists is corrosive, and it numbs the misled buyers who surrender to favor and disfavor alike. In recent years, cynicism has increased to an astonishing degree, just as propaganda has resorted to unimaginable methods. Art dealers write books and essays in which they praise the goods in their possession, often under a false name, in order to mislead the reader; they edit so-called magazines that are nothing other than catalogs of their business concerns; they form alliances with newspapers and magazines by means of advertising contracts in order to present their wares in the brightest possible light in search of purchasers. With very few exceptions, the critics are at their service. They are even in league with a state that is overburdened with debt and which is pleased to turn a blind eye if only they are granted a share of the profits. Speculation in artworks falsifies the market prices by means of the deceptive way in which prices are artificially driven upwards in public auctions. The consequence is that occurrences as obvious as those which prompted the development of Cubism have remained unknown to most of those who take part in these reckless dealings as onlookers, either through true ignorance or complacency or even sordid calculation. How many of the works written in the past few years about Cubism stood under the influence of the galleries and the reports of public sales, perhaps without their authors wanting this to be the case, because that was where the information came from? And yet, it would have been equally easy for them to go to the Bibliothèque Nationale and to read through the piles of newspapers from 1910, 1911 and subsequent years whose pages are not even yellowed, in order to read the authentic reports on this important historical movement.

It must be said: the continuous reassessments which have taken place in art circles since 1919 instill horror in the galleries. The artist, who more than anyone else should steer clear of economic considerations, has unwittingly become the agent of all this profiteering. His relationship to the dealer is untenable; the latter values him only inasmuch as he is a supplier. The confusion is immeasurable; what will happen if no one speaks out against this public auction of the intellect?

●

Let me now return to Cubism; it has continued to grow like a living plant, which is what it was beyond the commercial transactions in which the most visible products of the mind are distorted.

In January 1920, the artistic relationships between France and Germany were reinstated in an exhibition which I organized in Berlin, in the "Sturm" gallery of Herwarth Walden. That was when the magnificent work of the Polish artist Louis Marcoussis, who lives in Paris, could be seen in Germany for the first time.

During the same years, Fernand Léger, Georges Braque, the Pole Survage, the Russian sculptor Archipenko and I had the idea of reviving the "Salon de la Section d'Or" from 1912. A large exhibition was held in Paris and assembled a group of completely new works. It was impossible not to recognize in these convincing documents the extent to which the continued development of the idea had burst open the thin shell of the word Cubism.

A few months later, I published a small work, "Du Cubisme et des moyens de le comprendre." In it, I tried to draw up general principles, simple and clear elements, on which all authentic painting is based. The work is also known in Germany, because it was translated into German and an edition was published by "Der Sturm" in Berlin.

Since then, Cubism has followed its natural development, becoming increasingly established from year to year, protected by its own vitality against all commercial undertakings, and it has gradually spread from aesthetics across all aspects of life. Because this was the goal those timid experiments from the year 1911 aimed to achieve, which had had the rare advantage of causing an uproar in their surroundings: to position artworks once again in the midst of human life, reestablishing once more a link which had been broken since the Renaissance. And while aesthetic speculation wanted to recognize it only as a chance occurrence and a special case, the great speculation of practical life opposed it with a cruel denial by recognizing its ability to supply the elements of advantageous propaganda. I have no illusions about the true nature of this recognition; it is most definitely not without an interest in its own advantage. It does not know the striving for greater profundity which is interested only in quality; it is concerned with nothing but intensive production. However, it is psychological, because the whole of mankind is its clientèle, mankind in all its diversity, with its differences and its manifold reactions. Necessity has forced it to undergo an extraordinary training of its powers of reasoning. And therefore it clearly recognized the fundamental momentousness of Cubism, the force which it was able to exert on the crowd.

The huge speculation, in other words industry, production, and consumption, thus also moved in closer to Cubism and demanded that it cooperate. Let us say here immediately that they understood only the superficial impression of the new Cubist paintings that were on view in the art salons, the works of some older artists from 1911, who exhibited their works less and less frequently, and those of some younger artists who worked on its further development. They made use of the broad painting of surfaces, the interruptions to the continuous line; they adopted the angular drawing of descriptive outlines, and their use of color certainly imitated Cubist painting. They did not learn from the true Cubist painters but turned to artisans, skillful illustrators, poster painters. And so you could see Cubist-style advertisements on the walls in the big cities, furniture covers, dress fabrics, objects of all kinds in the big stores, increasingly simplified furniture with rigorous forms that focused entirely on essentials, and whose exclusive material contrasted with the intentional austerity of the appearance.

In this over-hasty application and wholesale translation which belong to the history of Cubism, I for my part recognize an indication of the significance of Cubism in the future. I had long had a premonition of this: today there can be no more doubt. Cubism was the first stage in the development of metaphysical painting, which was limited to the isolated painting on the easel — the inevitable finale of the Renaissance state of mind — to a secular painting called upon to have a share of architecture, as the re-burgeoning spirit demanded, which bore a strange resemblance to the Christian and whose forms the Romantic scholars were the first to rediscover.

In 1911, Cubism had actually begun with a reassessment of the idea of form, and thereby also with a reassessment of the concept of the painting. How many prejudices prevailed over this object! People were so accustomed to seeing the painting as one with the artist, and the artist seemed to be such an exceptional being that it became impossible to separate picture and artist. When one no longer meant the artwork, the artist was forgotten too, just as conversely the canonization of the painting secured at the same time the sanctity of the artist.

In the book which Jean Metzinger and I produced in 1912 with the title "Du 'Cubisme'," we had attempted to carry out a clear differentiation between the painting and decorative painting. We were content to define these two views of painting by simply contrasting them, without paying attention to their dependence on the attitude of the social milieu. Of course we granted the painting precedence. The development of Cubism would eventually supply us with a state which we would have seen as the worst solution at that time. In the changes that it underwent, Cubism proved to us that paintings and decorative painting are dependent neither upon personal opinion nor upon personal taste: Chardin and Cimabue did not need to decide. The state of mind of their time told the one to create a painting on an easel (tableau), and the other to create a mural (peinture décorative). Who would dare to maintain that one was less valuable than the other, simply with regard to the artistic quality? It was just that the state of mind of the time made one statement or another impossible with regard to painting. Only interim times like ours are inclined to choose between two attitudes; moreover, this too is also simply a delusion; because the coercion which leads the hesitant and the resistant towards the meaning of our life becomes increasingly clear.
Painting is always dominated and determined by architecture. Architecture expresses most clearly the mental state of a time. In it, we can follow the development of a human era and calculate its biological constants. Nothing gets lost in the social organism, but everything changes according to the stages of its growth. Thus we can say, taking painting into account, that if architecture controls the design of an era, then painting, as its servant, is dec⸗

orative. If, on the other hand, architecture falls into decay and is thus indicative of a reduction in the creative strength of the time, then this will have an effect on painting; it will break free of the order which is becoming powerless and, having to shift for itself, will develop into the panel painting. That is a finding which incidentally one can also make in dance, in music, in poetry and all literature, in sculpture and crafts. The Christian period has already brought once again the proof within the history of countless other epochs, whose human variations we are familiar with. The Renaissance demonstrated clearly the break between two mental states which correspond to the two prin= cipal ages of life; the first extends from birth to adulthood, and the second from adulthood to death. The first is constructive and the second is disinte= grating, in that it grants the organs a freedom which only appears to exist.

In the present state of mankind it is very easy to observe signs of insufficient coherence between organs, which are the prelude to the irrevocable dissolution of dated biological systems. On the other hand, with a degree of perspicacity we can recognize a striving for integration which would be the sign for a social realignment that is in the process of being formed: a struggle for primacy in the future is going on between the individual and the community. Within the area in which Cubism has had an effect I can see sure signs of a renewal of what was known as great decorative painting: the aesthetic production boldly encroaches on technical design and the descriptive painting on the living wall.

This untenable state, in which the spirit of society clashes with that of the individual, which grants the individual a misguided credit, runs counter to the attitude of many artists. It is opposed not only by those who under in= creasingly frequent appeals for help to the public disappear entirely in the darkness of a private law, but also certain Cubist painters of the early period who, incapable of abandoning a prejudice entirely, and without being com= pletely clear about it, return to the indecision of a Cézanne.

But what do we find so perplexing about decorative painting? Does it not bring freedom in conforming to laws? Is it for this reason that it fears the individual infatuated with himself will present himself in the spotlight? Char= acteristic of decorative painting are evidently the means of representation that have been invented and that are inexhaustible with regard to the technical possibilities. And so, by its very nature, technique determines the design.

As we can see immediately, it is now a matter neither of description nor of abstraction. It is a question of the assumption of a concrete fact, the creation of a reality of the same kind as in music, which stands on the bottom level of composition, and in architecture, which stands on the top step. Like every natural reality, painting that is understood thus will touch the soul of everyone who understands how to explore it, not on an indirect route via an opinion of creations that already exist, but through its autonomous being with all living relationships in which the whole of life is reflected.

The panel painting is considerably different. Since it has to do with a given object, it must subordinate the technical possibilities to a sensuous reproduction of foreign design elements. It can only permit an invention of means in an economical manner. The power of invention can only have an effect in the ambiguity of individual opinion; thus the painting gets lost in a formless description, and that all the more easily because it was never really formative in the true sense of the word. If you want to accept it at all in this state which signifies its complete demise, then you must allow the individual opinion without any form of restriction. On the day on which the artist was compelled to justify himself through his unusual way of seeing things, the painting had lost its sense for the general public; the increasingly strange transformations made it slip imperceptibly into the most abstruse metaphysics. In order to recognize this fact clearly, let us realize what the transformations of the painting offer us from the Renaissance to the present day; from Michelangelo, who painted it on a gigantic scale on a wall, to Braque and Picasso, who forced it into a restricted frame. We can see how the descriptive, in other words what man perceives through the window of his eye, is expressed in the first instance according to a general agreement based on normal perception, without stopping in the direction of individual perception of more uncontrollable personal assessment, in a word in order to slide in the direction of abstraction.

In the meantime, in the works of Braque and Picasso, who had pursued the independence of the artist to a very great extent during the first period of Cubism, we saw not only this decisive drive from the Renaissance. In their descriptive and atmospheric transformation, they came up against the fringe areas of picture resolution and two-dimensional geometry, which supported them on firmer ground. They dared to work with glued papers, with various materials, with sand, with marble dust, with imitations in fake wood and fake marble and with capital letters. Through this truly new function they contradicted the method of the Renaissance, which the artists had never given up completely since they depicted the outside of things metaphysically. All this passed, if not unnoticed, then at least not understood. And yet, it really would have deserved the consternation of the public, because in all seriousness there was a tangible threat that they would break with the panel picture. Instead, people had great fun with the transformation of the descriptive painting, which in no way jeopardized the future of painting as it prevailed in academic and independent circles. I even believe that most of them still assumed that Cubism was nothing more than a new sort of description, without having the slightest idea of what had definitively already reached pastures new before the very eyes of the world. In those new pastures lies the area in which painting is governed by technique, where the form applies for its own sake in its perfect form. But this was and still is all too easy for minds that recognize no progress except when it is complicated.

At any rate, these elements of reality, glued paper, sand, imitation wood etc., meant considerable boldness. They permitted an autonomous design to develop which as a result of the invented means of representation unfailingly led to a reintroduction of decorative painting. Painting within architecture, for the execution of which only craftsmen are required, is the continuation of the great decorative painting that was previously indispensable. This had to die after the Renaissance, when it no longer associated itself with the derelict architecture, and what little of it remained significant for the construction of meaning was left up to modest craftsmen. They stuck to technical rudiments because they gained no more inspiration from superordinate values. The feeble attempts that they undertook use descriptive imitation to raise themselves to the heights of artists, with whom they had had no connections at all since the seventeenth century, persuaded them to convey the failed illusion of wood and marble; this art was itself doomed to perish. But in that now Braque and Picasso undertook to introduce these modest imitative elements in the panel painting, they boldly began a work of renewal, above all with materials which indisputably belonged to the technique of the craftsman. They abandoned the opinion that had kept artists and craftsmen separate from each other: that the framed painting was intended for a privileged class of people and great decorative painting for everyone.

Metzinger, Delaunay, Léger, and I assessed the drawing that was accessible to all higher than Braque and Picasso on the one hand, but on the other hand were less inclined to be engulfed in metaphysical fog. We saw the essential in the verticality of the picture surface; beyond the analysis of description, which challenged us inwardly and outwardly, we ascribed a great constructive value to the overall composition. We wanted the viewers to gain initially an overall impression through the simple distribution of light and dark; the narrative inevitably had to give way to organized painting. We may believe that our efforts have been fairly successful, since people voiced the reproach in the first instance that a painting was incomprehensible. They were used to looking at a painting only for the story that it told them. We also went beyond the usual scope of a painting because we felt the easel was inadequate in the face of the boldness of the undertaking. A large surface was necessary so that the painting could achieve its full effect. The spaciousness was doubtless the cause of tech=nical changes. The brushstroke (touche), which made sense in a small painting, was a nuisance across the expanse of a large canvas. We have all had to struggle with its shimmering. Delaunay even used distemper and wax colors, difficult techniques, which would have been impossible for delicate brushwork in the style of Cézanne. And in that the form gradually returned to its surface context and again became creative, learned again to realize itself beyond the description of the space, the technique became two=dimensional again, freed from the complications which the cult of the panel painting had led it into. It finally became capable of expressing the reality of a living composition as the spirit demanded it, and by using their eyes every viewer could become aware of which social category he too belonged to, and which intellectual skills he had at his disposal. Because this reality is not the prerogative of a few; it belongs to everyone, and everyone can get something from it, depending on his strengths. This insight is not new: it is also the origin of the myth of Orpheus, whose song moved animals and plants in the same way as people. Just as now the artist retreated before the craftsman and decorative painting outgrew painting, so metaphysics had to give way to reality, and the idea of the image was brought back to life.

All the Cubist artists advanced towards the organization of decorative paint=ing. The means invented in view of the technical possibilities prevailed to the disadvantage of perspective, that miserable means of controlling description.

However, the prejudices disappeared so slowly that most of these painters were almost ashamed of the results of their investigations, instead of making use of them openly as their invention. Since decorative painting fell into disrepute, it seemed disgraceful to them as artists to have anything to do with it. The great epochs of art, whose wonders they praised at the same time — also one of the usual inconsistencies of today's interim age — and which were dominated by architecture and subsequently by sculpture and decorative painting, could not convince them that they were only the victims of habit. And I believe I am not wrong when I maintain that these painters are still not fully aware that they have reestablished an order which is necessary for our time and have achieved greatness through its anticipation.

Business applications and exploitation understood this better than they did, for the simple reason that commerce in its most general and consequently most essential interest did not address a supposed élite, but rather as large a society as possible. It therefore recognized the full extent of the advantage which it could derive from the newly invented means of representation, a consequence of the technical possibilities. It recognized the extent to which the imagination of the crowd could be stimulated by the enormous attraction of completely new forms. And the necessary result was that it adopted Cubism in its goals and its technique. Today, when people continue to disparage Cubist painting and to describe it as a huge mistake, they are nonetheless united everywhere in the recognition that "the aesthetic movement which has changed modern taste, can be traced back to real painting, with which it basically had nothing to do. Cubism is indeed the current style for everything that starts anew. Whereas in pure art it evidently means nonsense." I took up this quote by chance from a provincial newspaper, where I had recently read it — the Lyon Républicain of February 9, 1928 — but it is similarly the leitmotif which you can find everywhere, as soon as people start talking about so-called modern aesthetics. While we are compelled to determine what cannot be overlooked, at the same time we become set on the contradictory assertion that the starting point for these phenomena is an error. However, we distinguish this lesser art from the special case of the higher form; in other words, life in all its facets, the life of the people as a whole is not real life, but its denial.
Thus Cubist painting alone can hold its own within all these attempts being made in all fields where industry exercises its power. Modern decorative artists

are by no means fully aware of this fact. However, if an architect with sufficient energy appears in order to become the master workman of former times — and sooner or later he will come, as the period of decline of the old mental state already bears the seed of this — then of necessity he will have to apply to the Cubist artists as soon as it is a question of painting. And so we must come to the conclusion that Cubism has torn down the dividing walls which separated total art from that supposedly purer form of panel painting. When hitherto errors reigned supreme on this matter, then it was simply up to those who had not noticed that in order to be able to launch a fresh start after all, the entire Occident began to change its mental state by renewing modern tastes.

●

These are the major changes in appearance up to the present day which were described as Cubism about 17 years ago. The men whose names I have mentioned did not realize the immense importance of their work at that time. And even less did they have an inkling of the repercussions which their experiments would subsequently have, and that they would finally surpass themselves.
So Cubism was not a strange incident in the more or less regularly ascending curve of painting. Numerous writers have attempted to interpret it in order to demonstrate its justification or to show it as undesirable, depending on their own personal taste. All too much literature, both good and bad, has been created about it without revealing its true nature; the painters have also placed more value on defending their personal opinion than on openly admitting that here it was perhaps a matter of rediscovering a world beyond their powers. Impudent lies were disseminated out of material interest, out of a fear of having to confess one's own bankruptcy. What is the message behind all these trivialities that belong to everyday life? Life consists not only of opposites; it also knows how to dispel them, and after many years, living Cubism has been recognized. Because life and technique agree in their rejection of the aesthetics of pure art.

The Art Déco exhibition in Paris in 1925 supplied the best evidence for the rewards of continuing to hold firm to Cubism. The exhibition proved its external influence in the more superficial form of business applications and exploitation. When the first account is given of the fact that Cubism is not

only a matter of seeing, then people will take the trouble to study its funda⸗
mental principles and will no longer be satisfied with external appearances.
Only then can the basis of a new creative drive be appreciated. The question
will remain, however: in which direction will the new design develop with
time?

Until then, Cubism will have to limit itself to working towards its perfection.
If the men who deserve the fame of having established it should lose their
drive after all the battles which so far have only led to ceasefires, then younger
ones will step into their shoes; some are already there, serving the cause with
new strength and the same commitment.

The series of reproductions which illustrate this work enable the reader to gain
a proper idea of Cubism in modest but adequate measure, and to acquire
a picture of its development since 1911. He will see there the old artists from
the beginnings, from the first period of the new creation of the form, who
tackled the volume, then moved on to the analysis of the outward appearances
of the object, before finally arriving at a synthetic expression. Furthermore,
in the interests of completeness I have also allowed the young artists to take
their rightful place: we can see which sides of Cubism they consider to be
important, so that they in turn could continue to develop them. And doubtless
he will sense the last realizations of the reassessments of the Renaissance
idea of form, which was static and descriptive, then slowly became transformed
in order to finally end in a new lively and concrete formal idea. Robert
Delaunay had anticipated it intuitively in 1913. The great decorative painting
of all religious ages, which remained under the direction of architects because
it was interested in construction, always assumed in its realizations this for⸗
mal idea which was conjectured by the Romantic scholars. That is also why
these periods were the eras of the epic, the song of rousing might; as soon
as the epic soul ceased to inspire the time which had arrived at the pinnacle of
its development, the period began which introduced our Renaissance.
So, with Cubism, the great decorative painting returned; and there was, as a
consequence, a revival of the epic.

1928

ILLUSTRATIONS

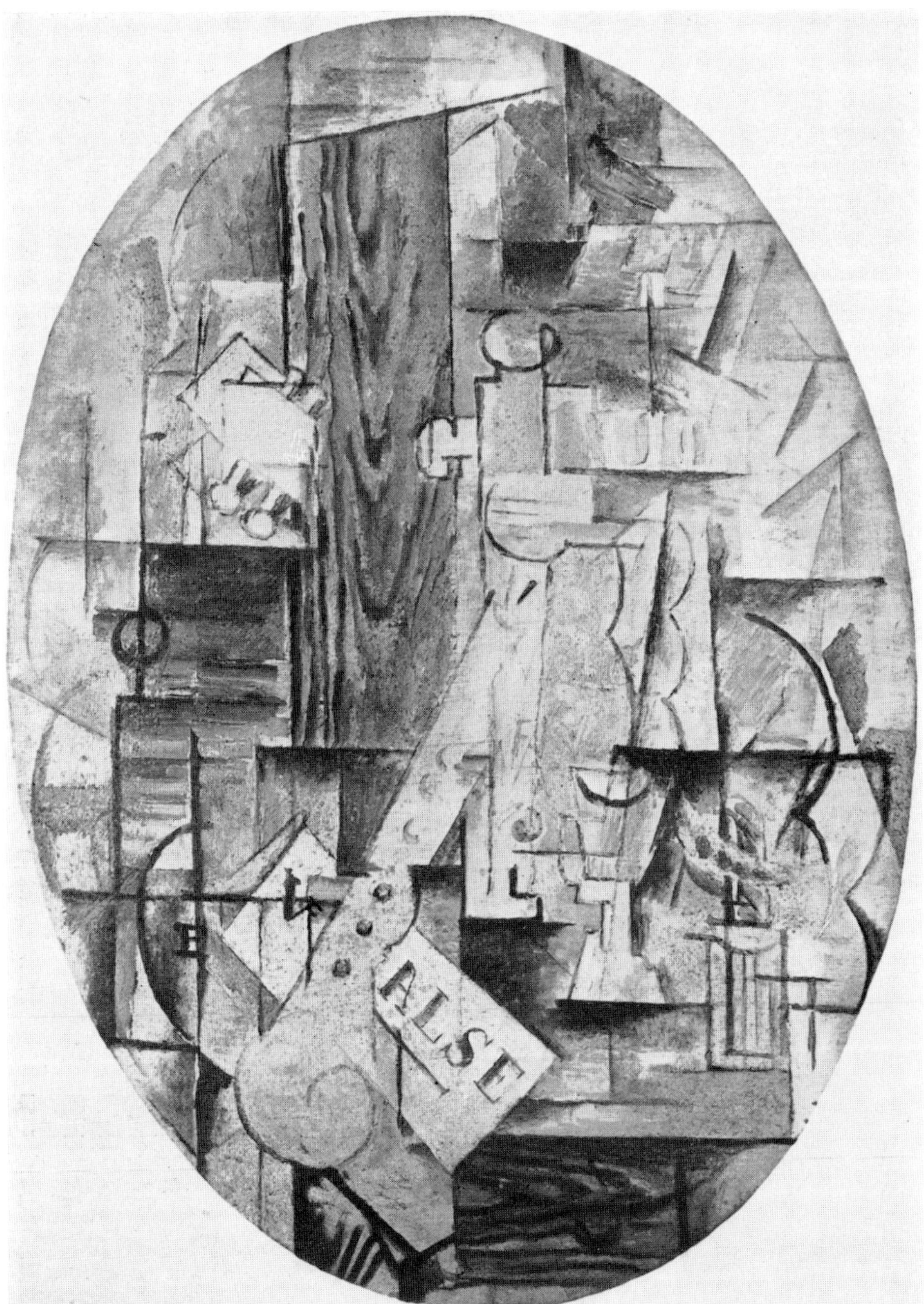

Fig. 1 GEORGES BRAQUE   OVAL STILL LIFE.   1913

Second stage of Cubism. In the earlier paintings, Braque studied the mechanism of volume in painting, the artistic illusion. Here he dispenses with volume. The descriptive element is traced back to geometric extension. Significance of the original surface, which determines the directions of the organic sections chosen by the artist. In contrast to the production of the panel painting, the craftsmanship of the mural painter. Braque's father owned a studio for mural painting. What Braque introduces into the artist's painting can be explained through the impressions of his youth; he influences Picasso, who grew up in museum maintenance — his father was a Professor at the École des Beaux-Arts — and introduces the renaissance of mural painting. It is here and in no other area that the boldness of his paintings lies.

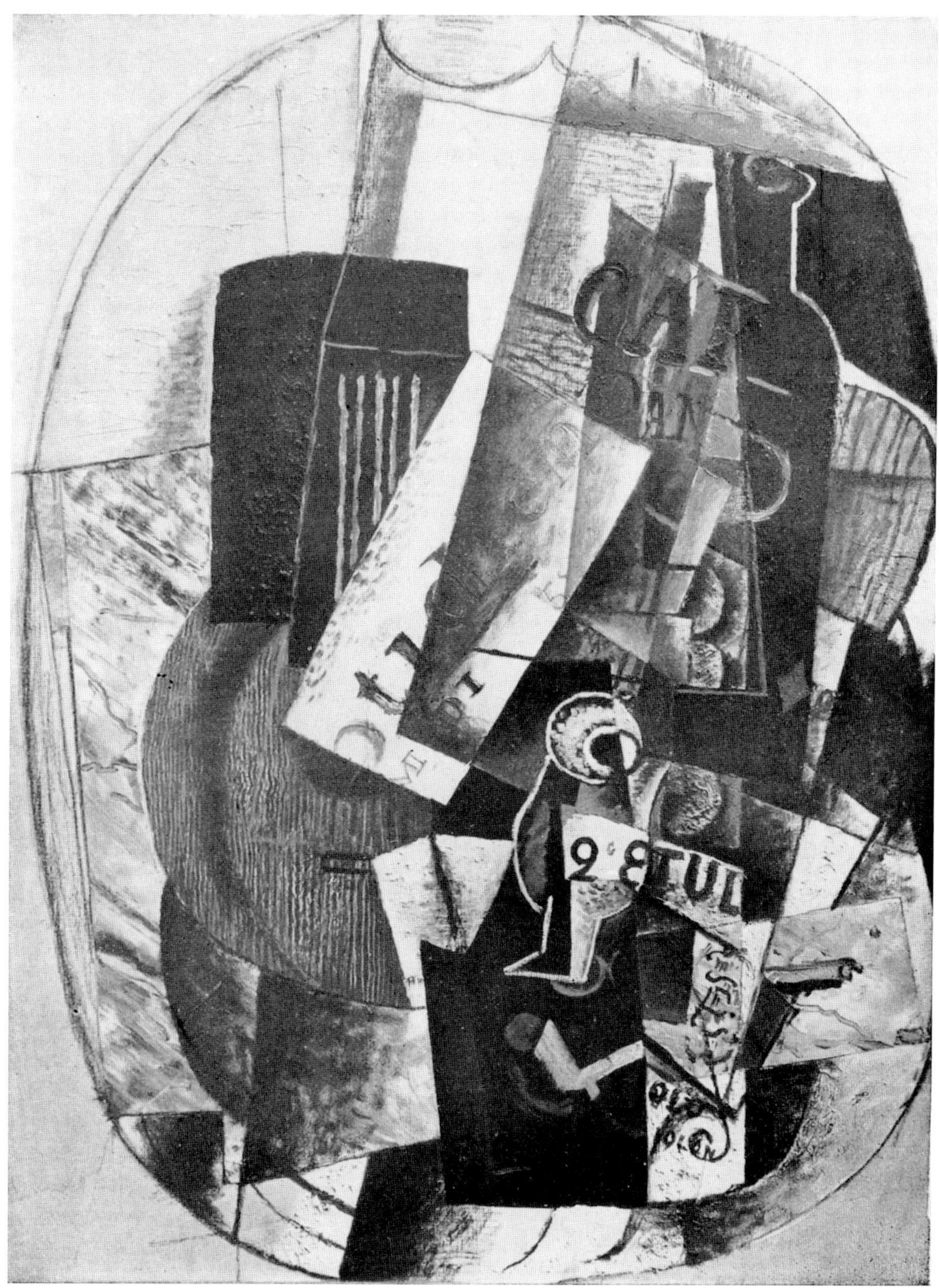

Fig. 2 GEORGES BRAQUE STILL LIFE. 1914

Second stage of Cubism. Another example of what has been said about Fig. 1. The verticality prevails over depth perspective. The essence of painting lies in the surface. The imagination submits to being led by rhythm.

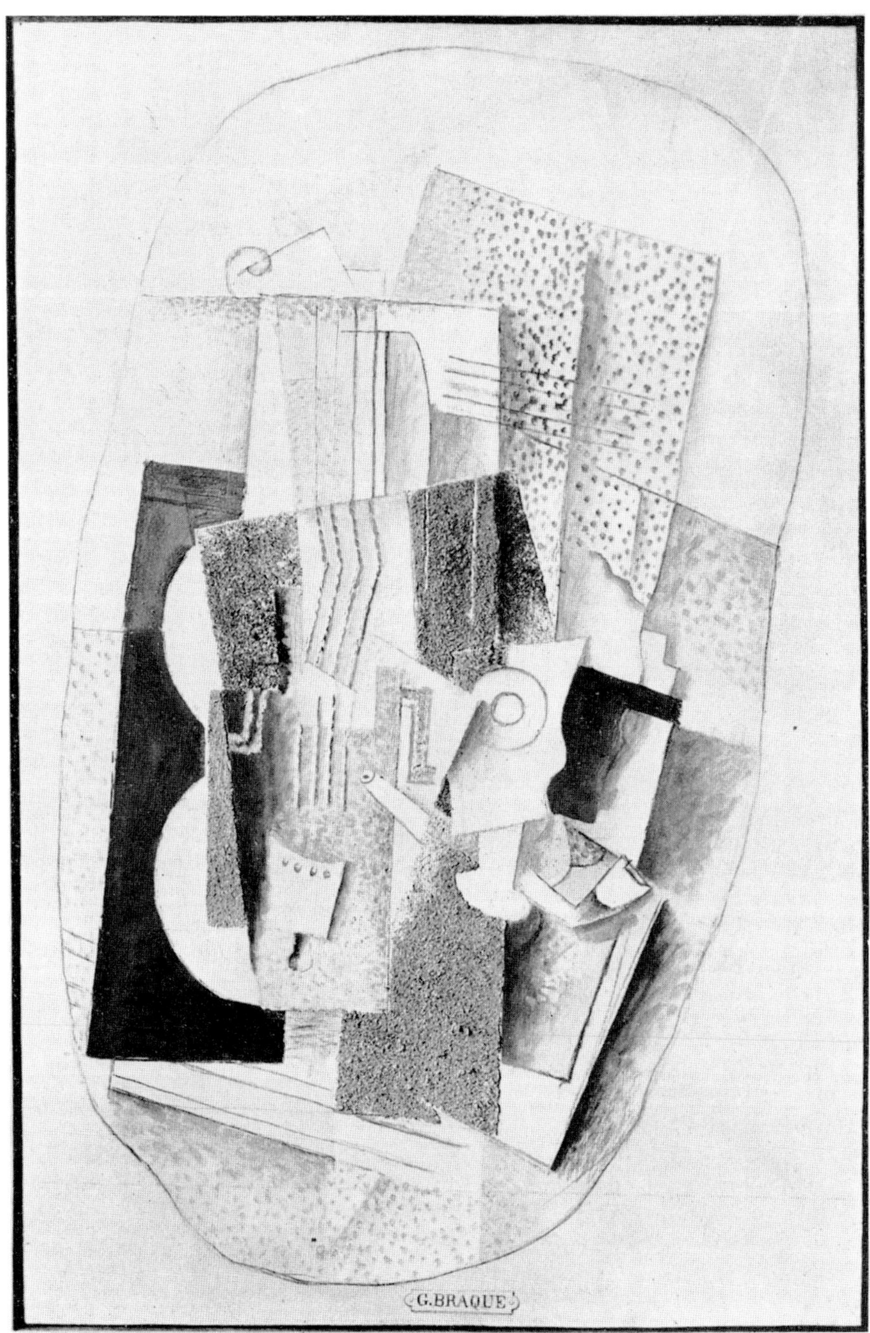

Fig. 3 GEORGES BRAQUE STILL LIFE. 1914

Third stage of Cubism. Simplicity, purity, cadenced rhythm. It is remarkable how the line is reintroduced as a means of design, prepared by the point from which it arises. The form is linear and envelops the substance. In painting, the plane is qualified by the substance, which in turn is enveloped graphically by the form.

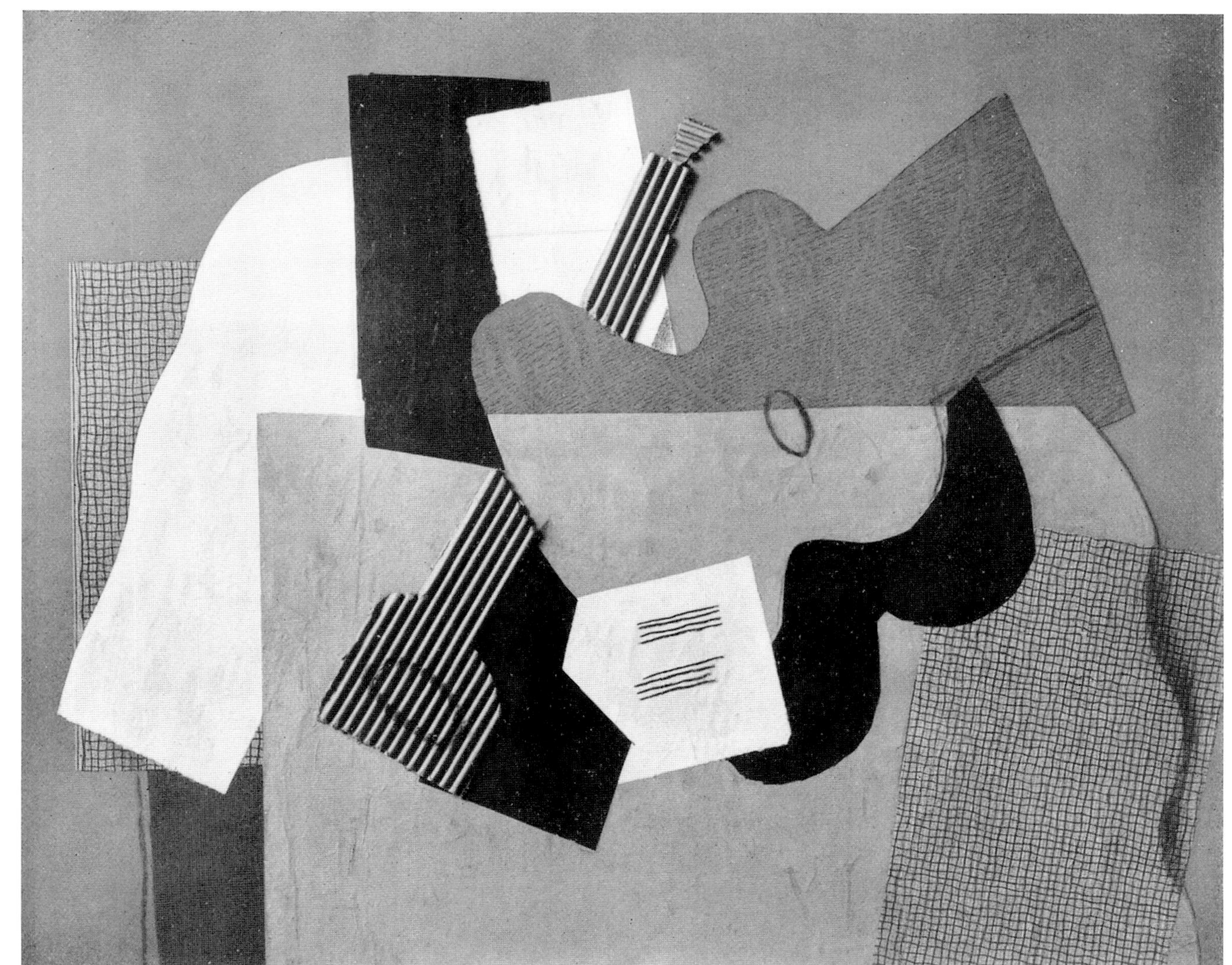

Third stage of Cubism. The planar elements are less numer=ous; the mobile form is empha=sized to a great=er extent. The contrasting ma=terials are more clearly opposed to each other, as a result of which the con=centration is more marked.

Fig. 4 GEORGES BRAQUE STILL LIFE. 1918

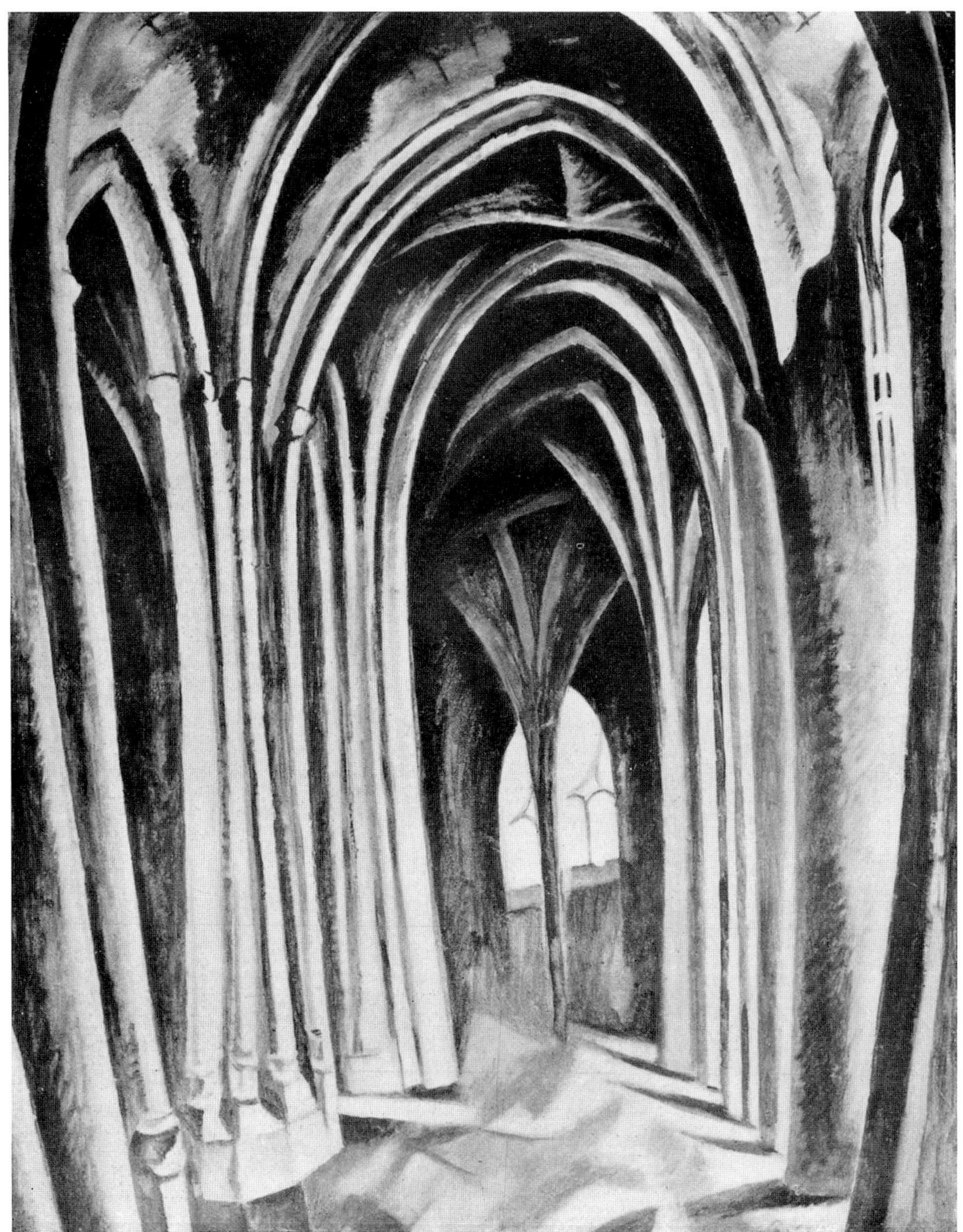

First stage of Cubism. Here Delaunay treats an extremely important optical problem purely instinctively, regardless of the reassessment of the volume: the deformation of the verticals from the observer's point of view. Medieval architects recognized the problem and knew how to solve it; during the Renaissance it was forgotten and not included in the calculation.

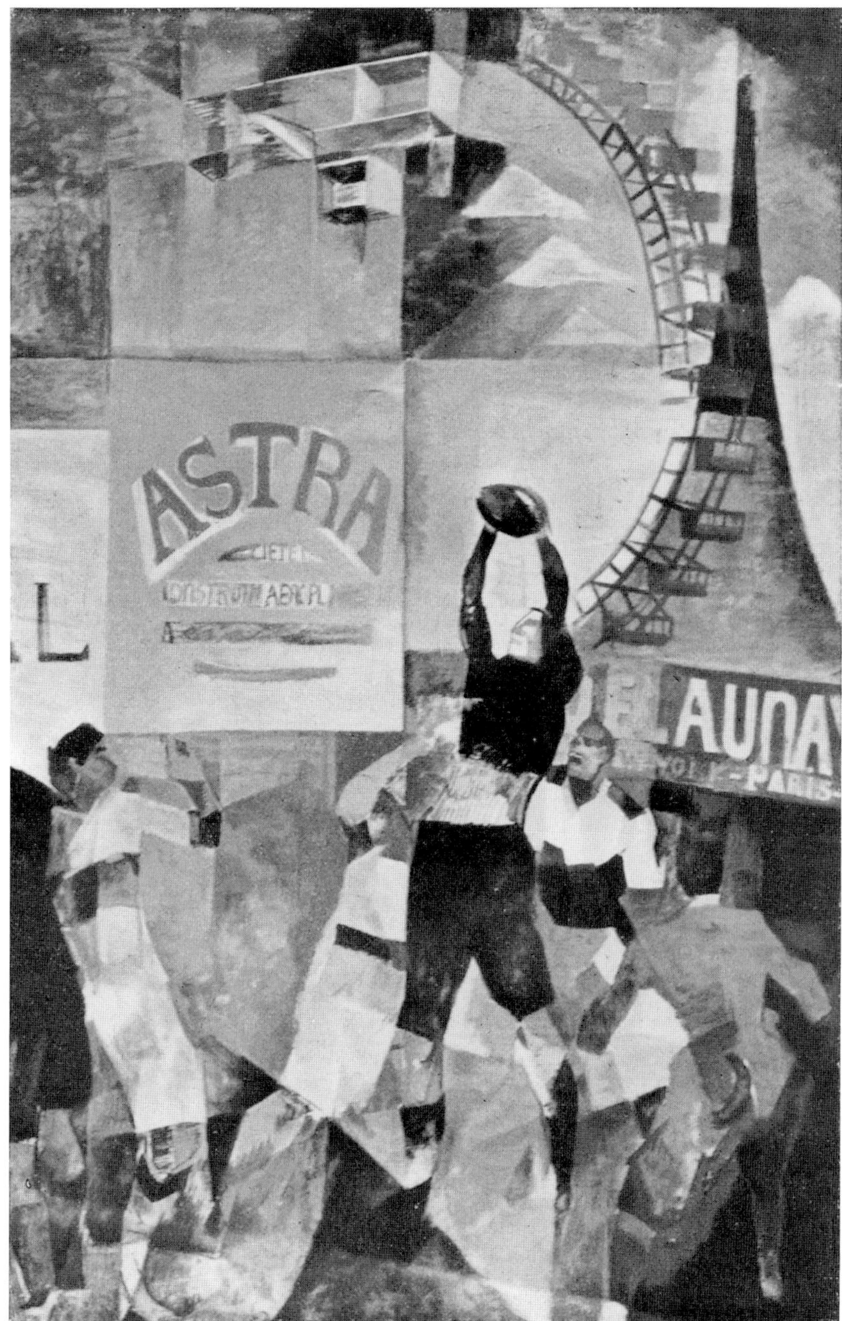

Fig. 6 ROBERT DELAUNAY THE CARDIFF TEAM. 1913

Second stage of Cubism. The descriptive form of the unity of perspective has been suspended. Delaunay gives the colored surface priority over the dominance of volume. Here he is exclusively a painter. He creates movement through the effect of the colors, on the one hand because of their particular nature, and on the other relative to their importance on the surface. The entire area of the canvas has been divided into a specific number of individual surfaces which are in lively interrelationship simultaneously or successively, corresponding to the power of their original nature.

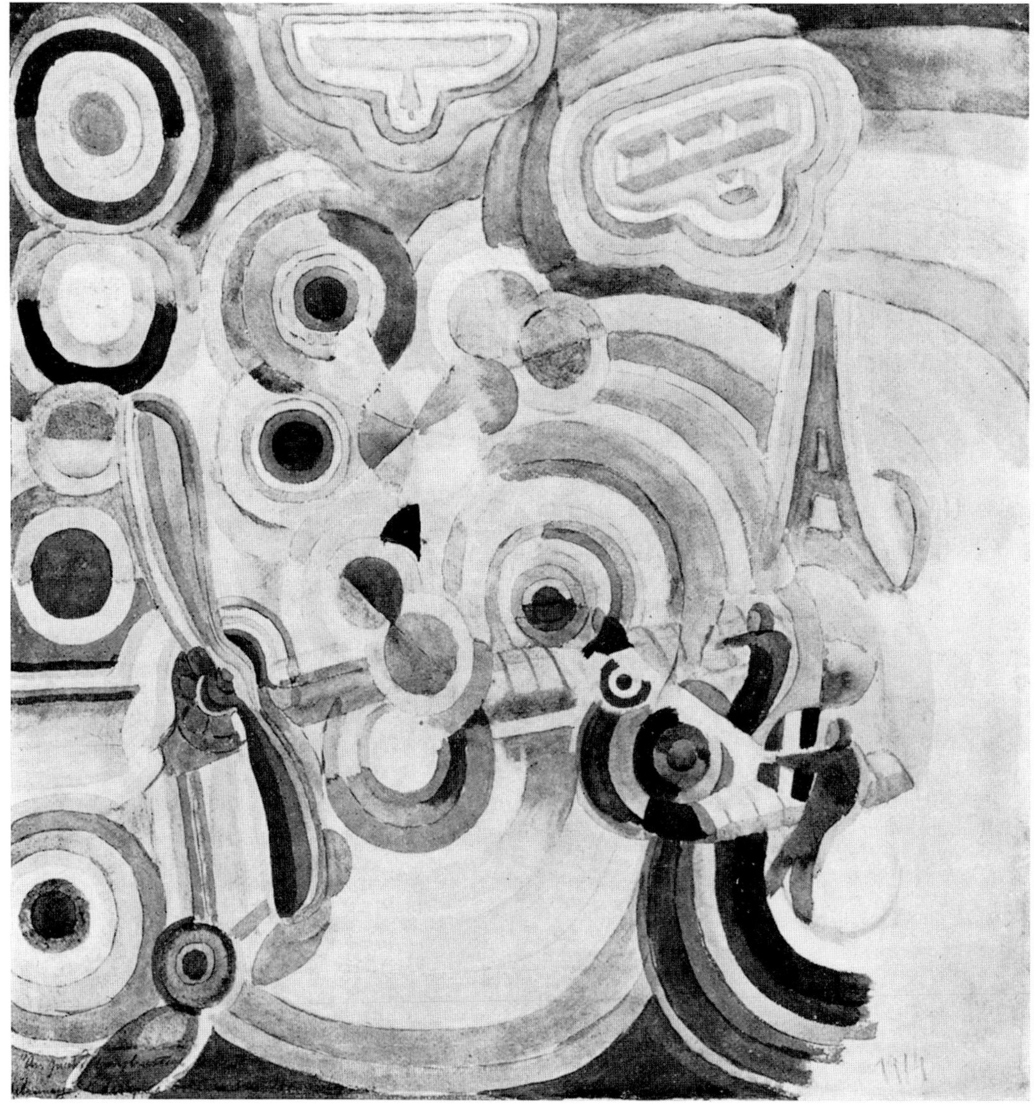

Fig. 7 ROBERT DELAUNAY SIMULTANEOUS CIRCLES. 1914

Third stage of Cubism. Here we observe the flexible mentality instead of the static one. A gyrat﹦
ing expression of form, undoubtedly still visual, but would anything else have been possible in 1914?
Form is movement, proclaimed Delaunay. Not a matter of opinion, not a matter for literature. Design
is movement in time. Color is a means of construction. The activity of the colors has only one
goal: to return to their origin, light; translated into a human relationship: to gray. Here lies the
fundamental problem of color. You do not progress from gray to color, but from color to gray.

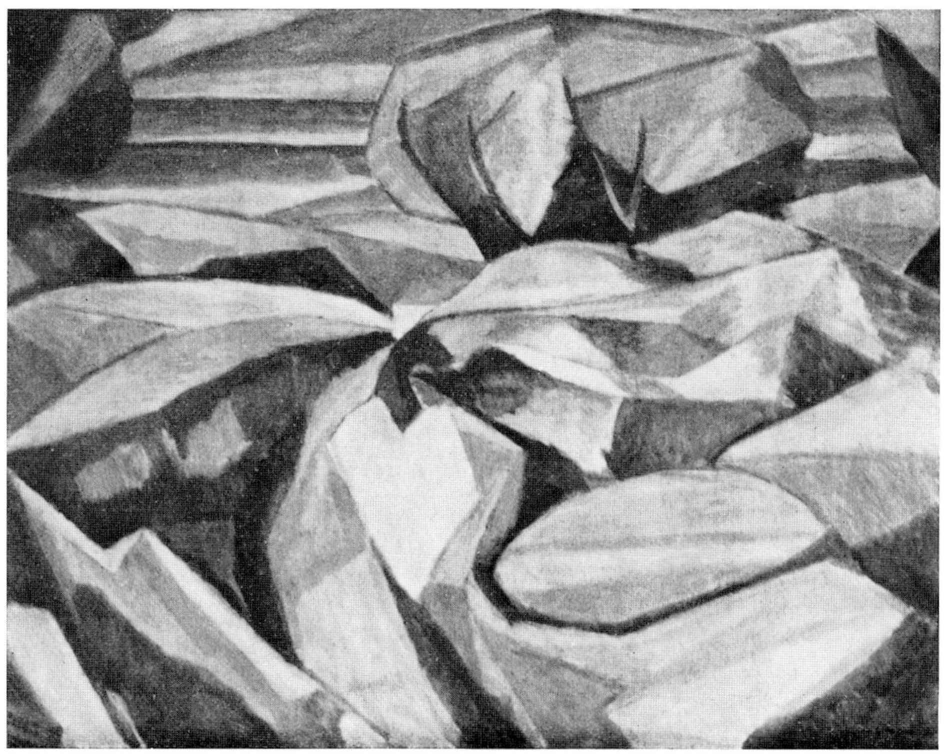

First stage of Cubism. Mechanism of volume: the unity of perspective is not in doubt. The descriptive anecdote is traced back to a scheme. The color is sacrificed to the nuances of gray.

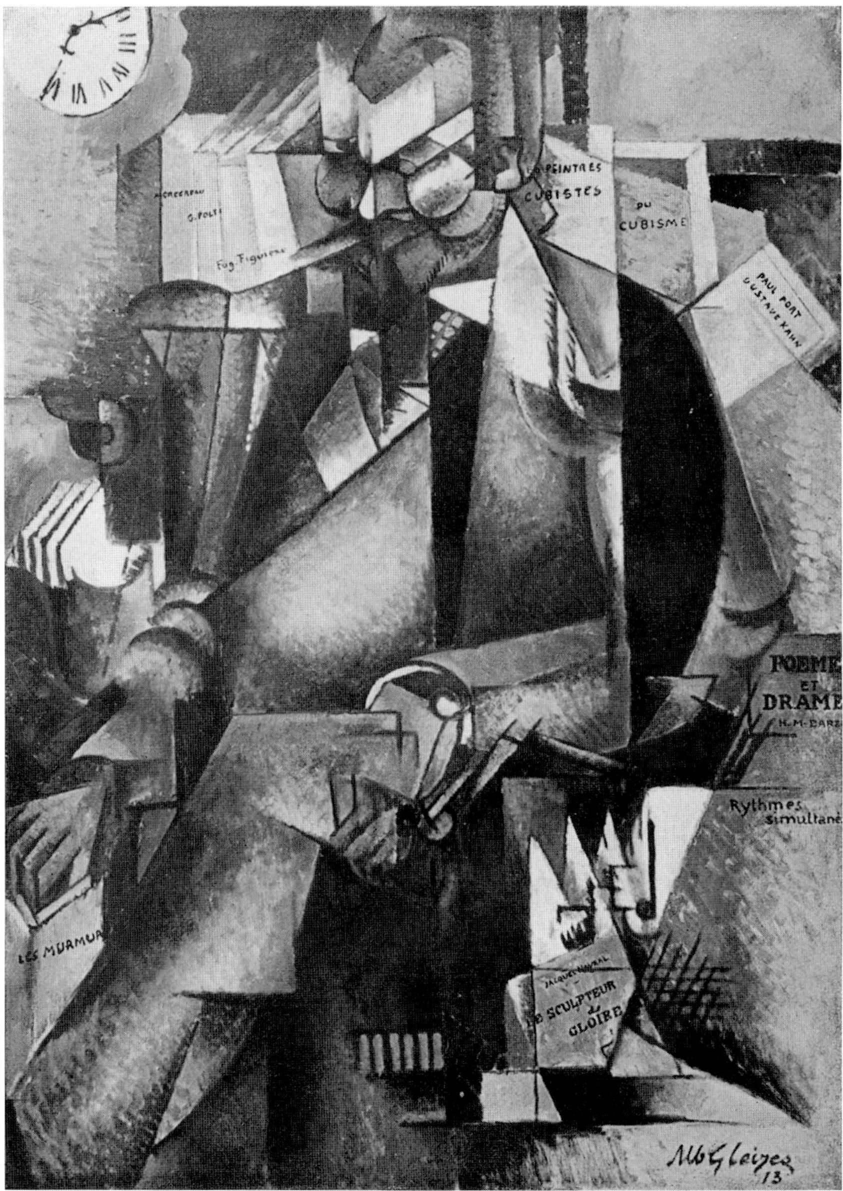

Fig. 9 **ALBERT GLEIZES** PORTRAIT OF THE PUBLISHER FIGUIÈRE. 1913

Second stage of Cubism. An attack on the Renaissance perspective. Multiplicity of perspectival points of view. The volume is suppressed by the importance of the plane. The description is divided into an intuitive order, subjected to the directions of the image limits. The careful little colorations are absorbed into the expansive entity of the gray.

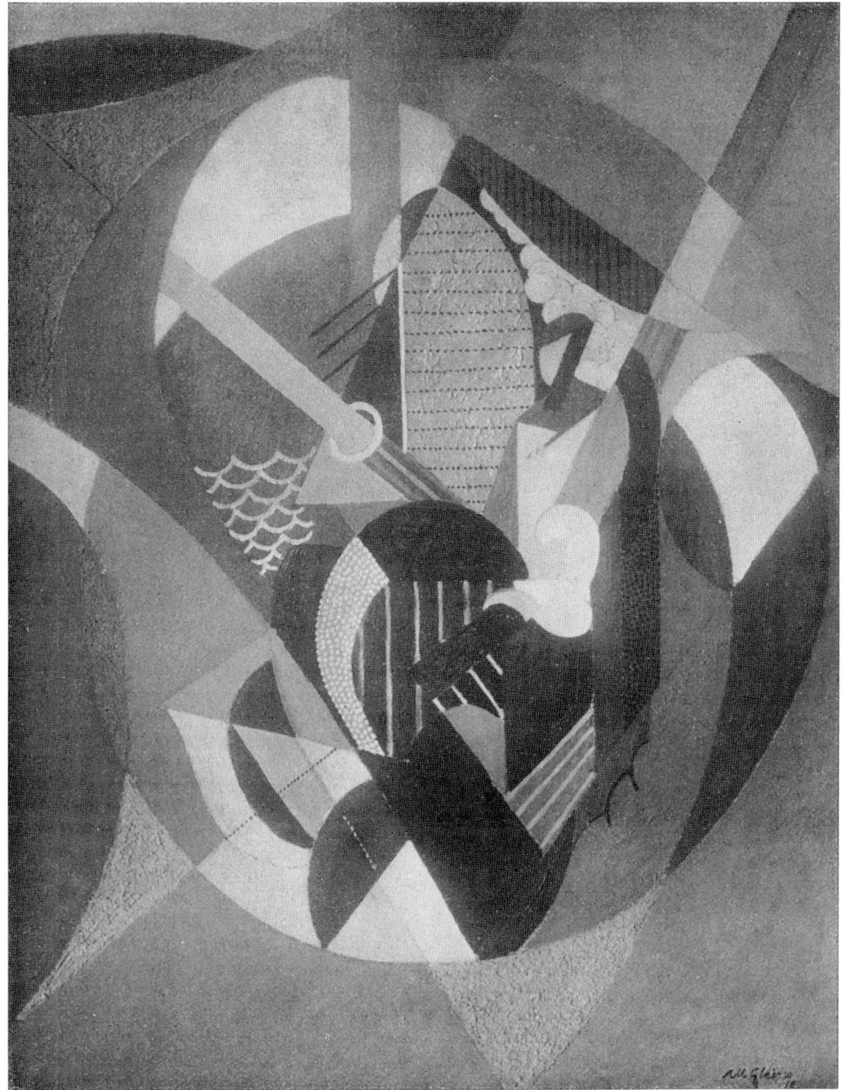

Fig. 10 ALBERT GLEIZES SAILING SHIP. 1916

Third stage of Cubism. Multiplicity of perspectival points of view. Volume, a description adapted to the nature of the surface. Here the distribution of colors is subjected to a system of design whose unity obeys new laws. A versatile rhythm gains in importance and the form of the circle urges expression. The color is deter=mined by the tonality of the overall surface of the picture. The paint application strives towards gray.

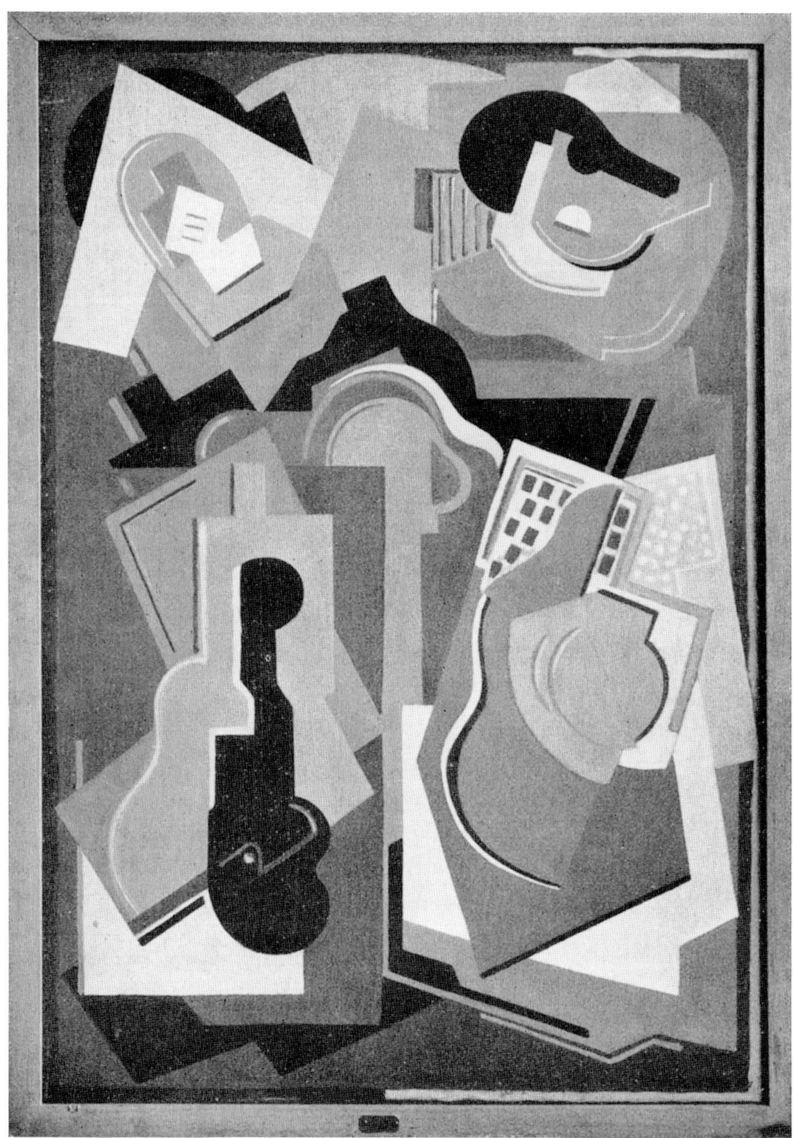

Fig. 11 ALBERT GLEIZES WALL PAINTING IN MANY BASIC FORMS. 1925

Further development of Cubism. Architectural design system; towards large-format wall painting; still on an individual level, but with the possibility of developing into a monumental total composition. The spatial form of the Renaissance confronts the temporal form of the Age of Religion.

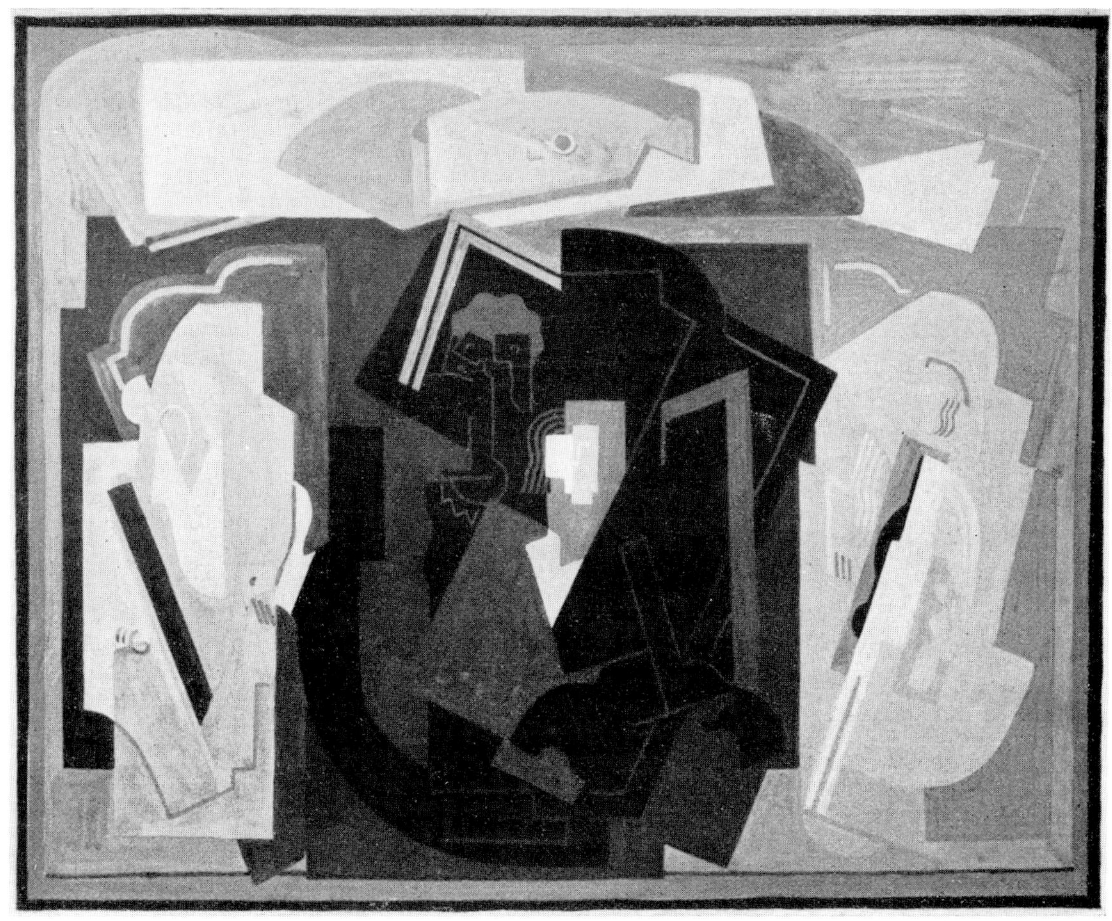

Fig. 12 ALBERT GLEIZES WALL PAINTING IN MANY BASIC FORMS. 1926

Another example of a design system with diverse rhythms, painted using the technique of a craftsman. Temporal form in contrast to the descriptive spatial form.

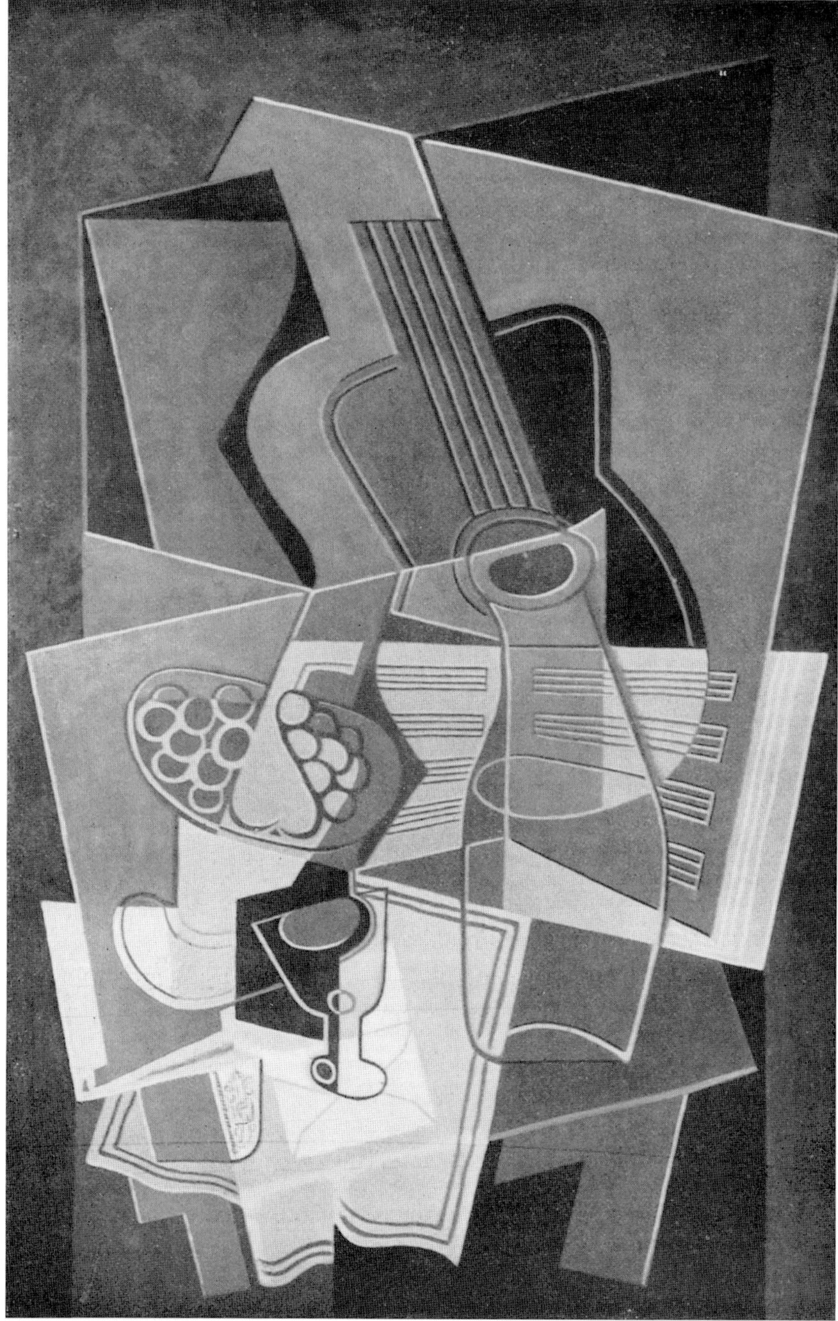

Fig. 13 JUAN GRIS STILL LIFE. 1921

Third stage of Cubism. Outstanding example of this stage, in which the new design system as opposed to the description of the Renaissance is clearly expressed. Gris has progressed through the second stage of Cubism, the logical struggle against the Renaissance dogma. Here he shows with rare clarity all the dynamic powers of the plane in their displacement and rotation. He communicates the concept of the circling form governed by time not only for the eye, but also for the intellect.

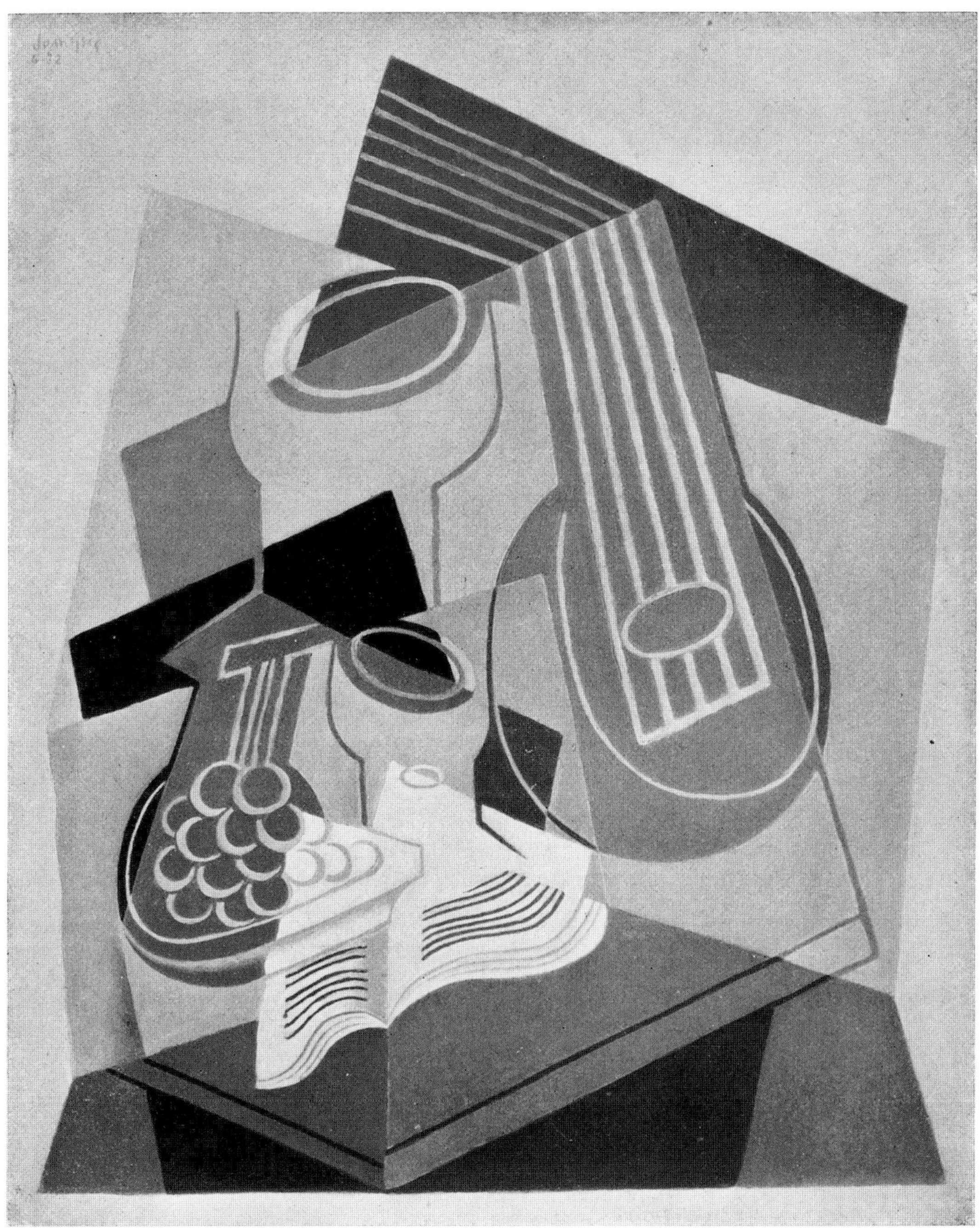

Fig. 14 JUAN GRIS STILL LIFE. 1922

Another fine example of the third stage of Cubism; the clarity of the temporal form is certainly evident here: do we not feel the epic power with which it imposes itself on the intellect through the intervention of the eye?

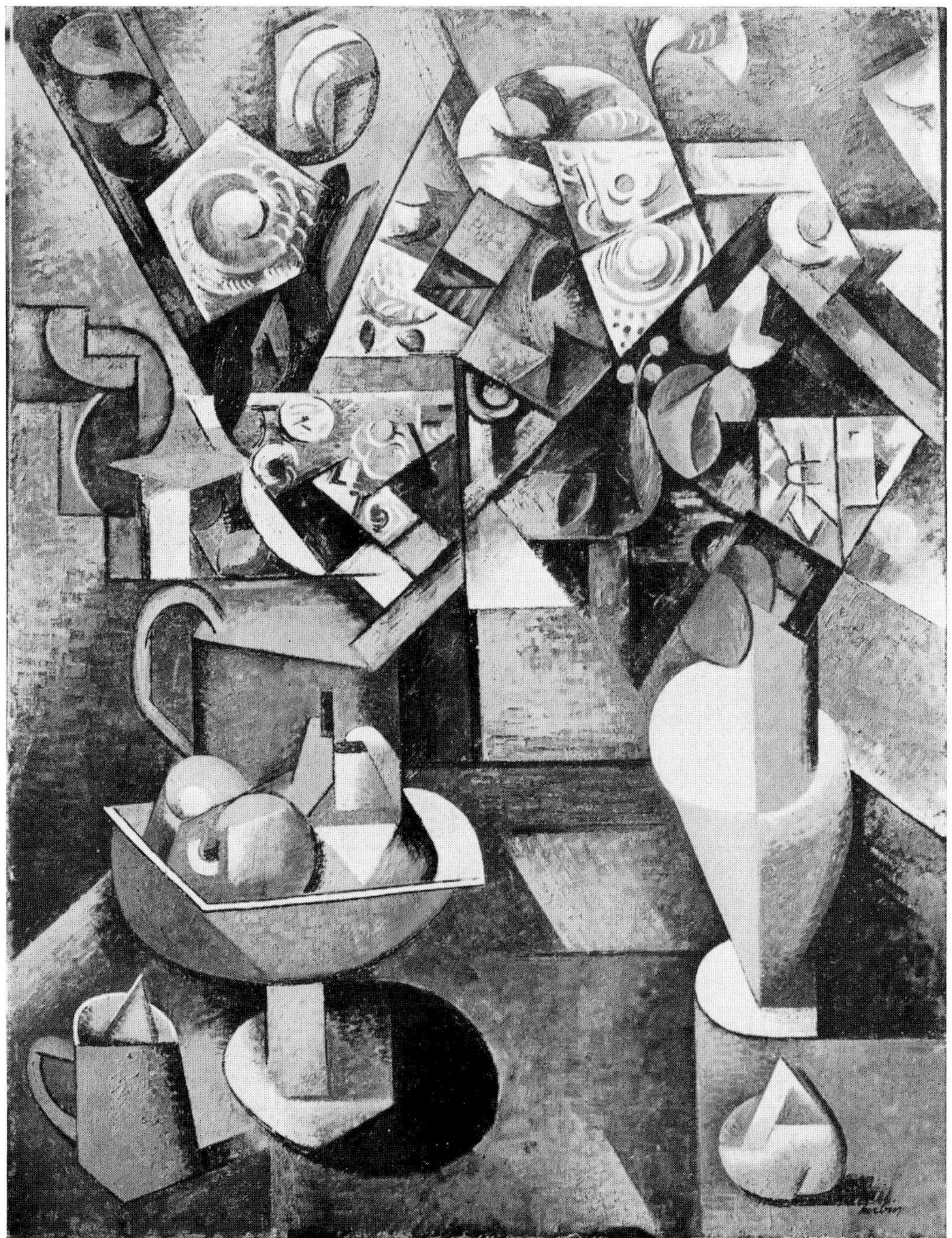

Fig. 15 AUGUSTE HERBIN STILL LIFE. 1912

Second stage of Cubism. An attack on perspective — multiplicity of perspectival points of view — the volume disappears behind the significance of the surface. Descriptive sections. Paint application in small areas. Herbin has passed through the first stage of Cubism, that of volume.

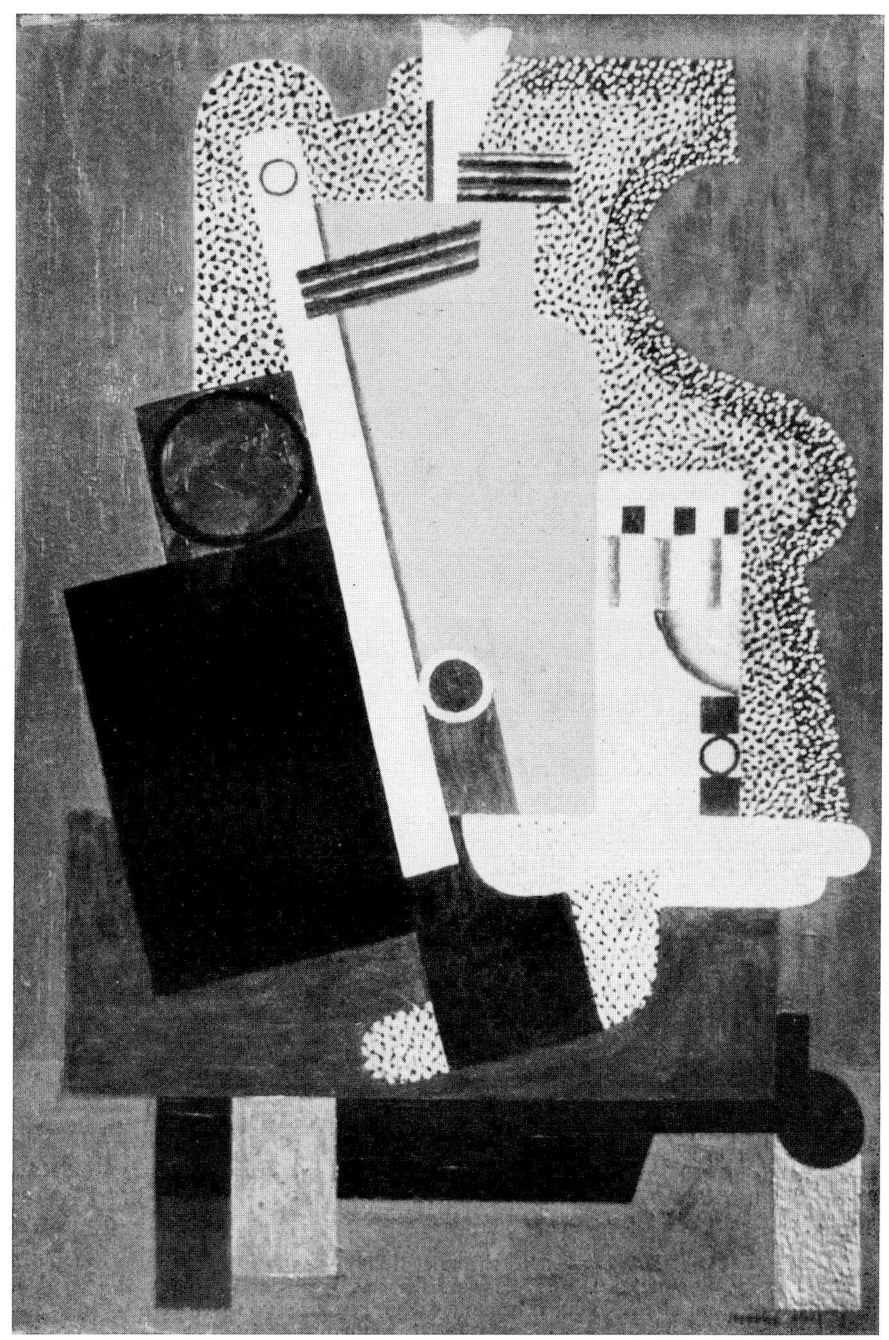

Fig. 16 AUGUSTE HERBIN STILL LIFE. 1919

Third stage of Cubism. The new system of temporal composition is expressed in this painting. The rhythm of the movement is tangible.

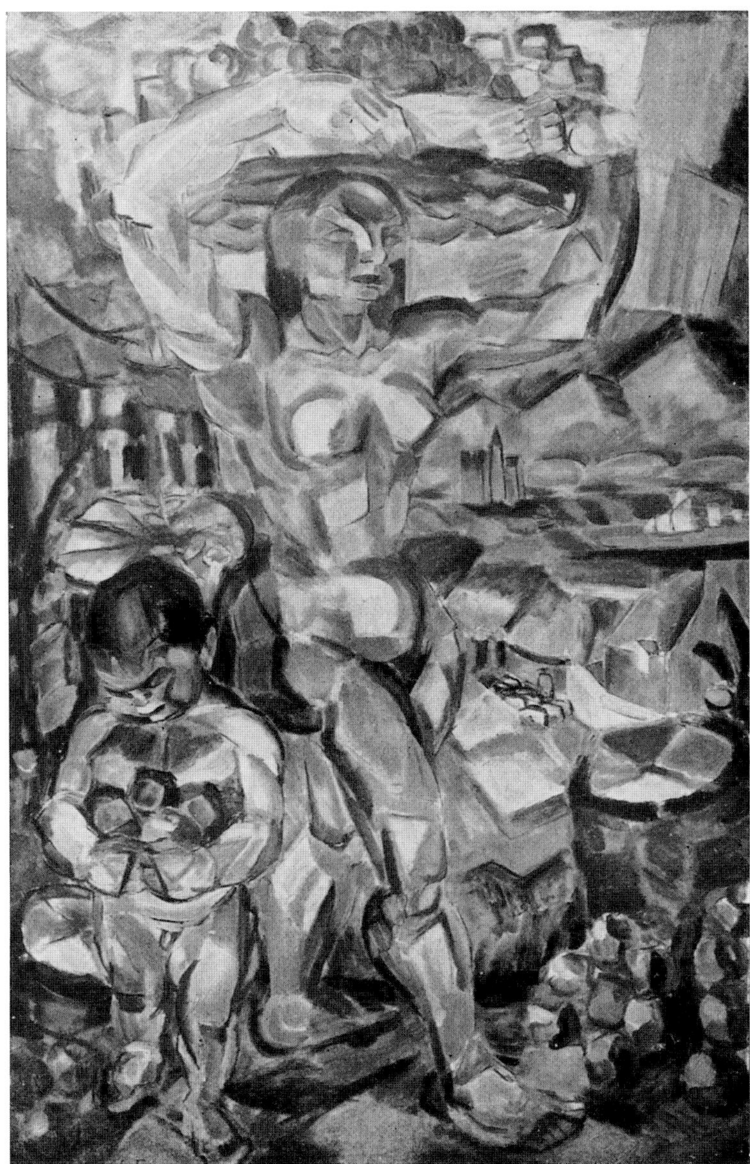

Fig. 17 LE FAUCONNIER FERTILITY. 1910

First stage of Cubism. A very fine example of the reassessment of volume. The perspectival unity is not questioned. The descriptive anecdote is only a pretext for the interplay of volumes, the crystallographic constructions, the contrasts between gravity and density. The color is drowned in a gray which is experienced directly as an essential component of the painting.

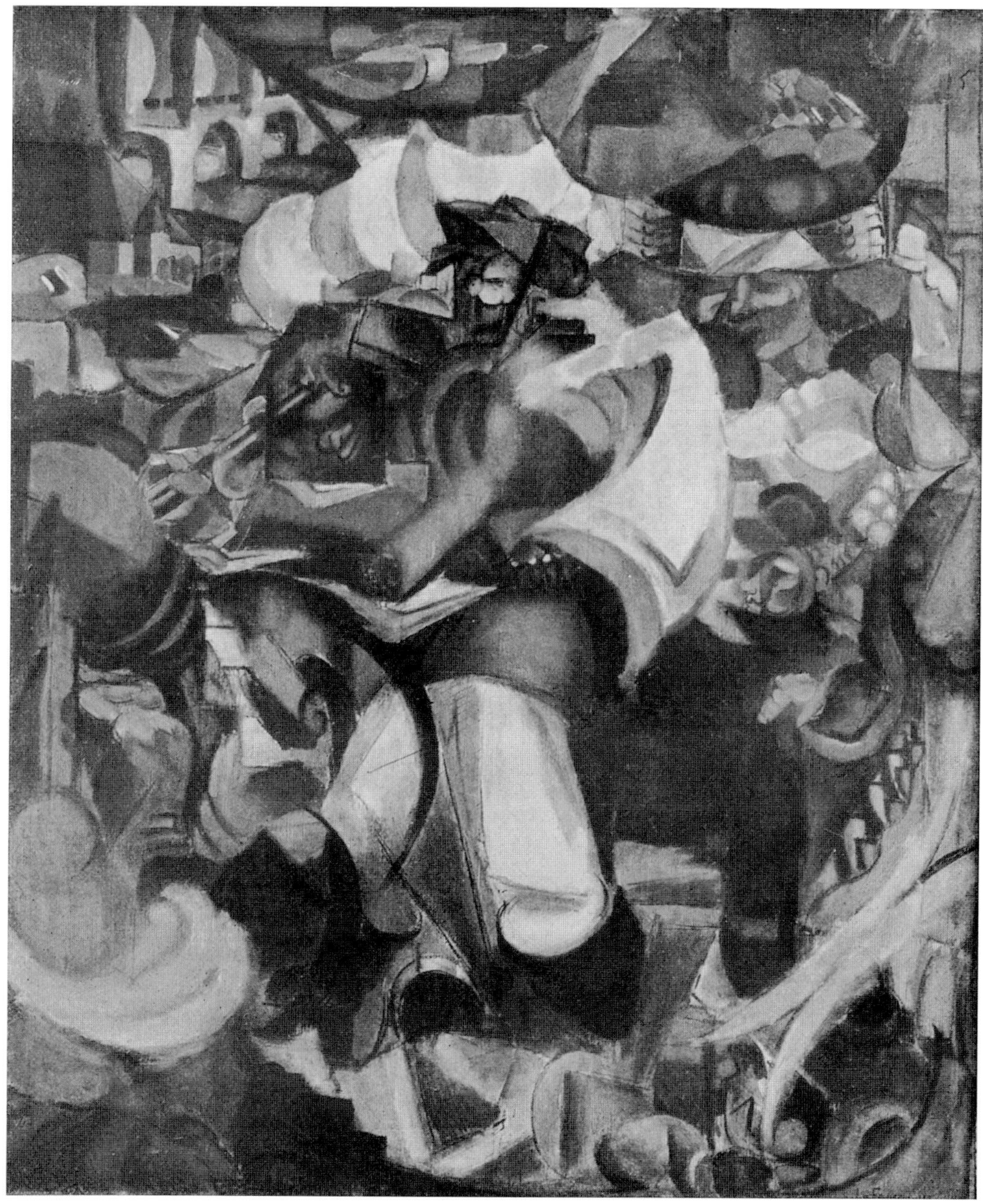

Fig. 18 LE FAUCONNIER THE HUNTER. 1911

Second stage of Cubism. One of the masterpieces of this era. All the problems have been dealt with: volume, perspectival shift, circular arrangement, rhythmical repetitions. Presses forward towards the goal of a new creative order, which corresponds to the attitude based on the mobility of the world.

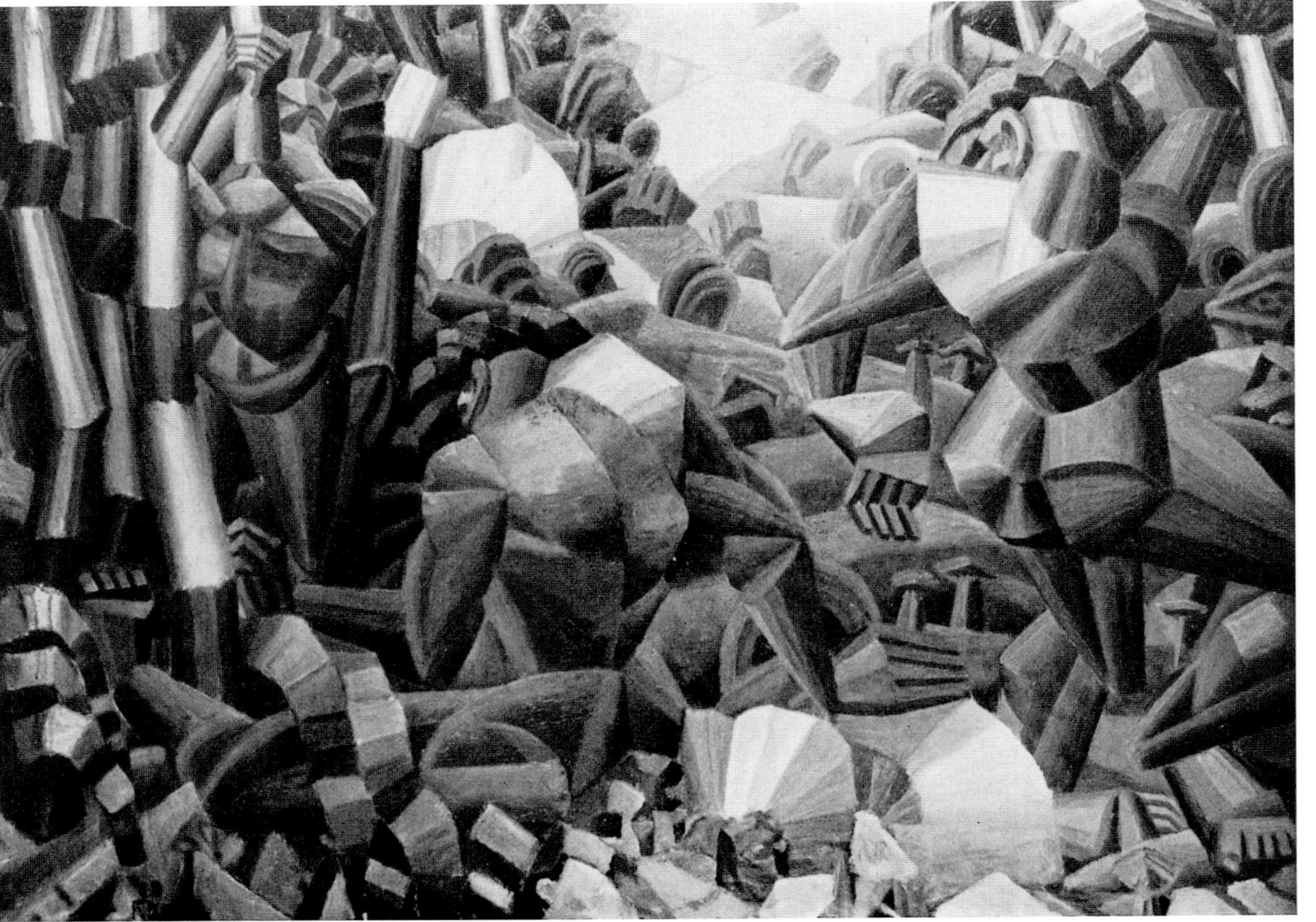

Fig. 19 FERNAND LÉGER   NUDES IN THE FOREST.   1911

First stage of Cubism. Mechanism of volume. The perspectival unity of the Renaissance is preserved everywhere. Schematically descriptive anecdote. Colors sacrificed to shades of gray.

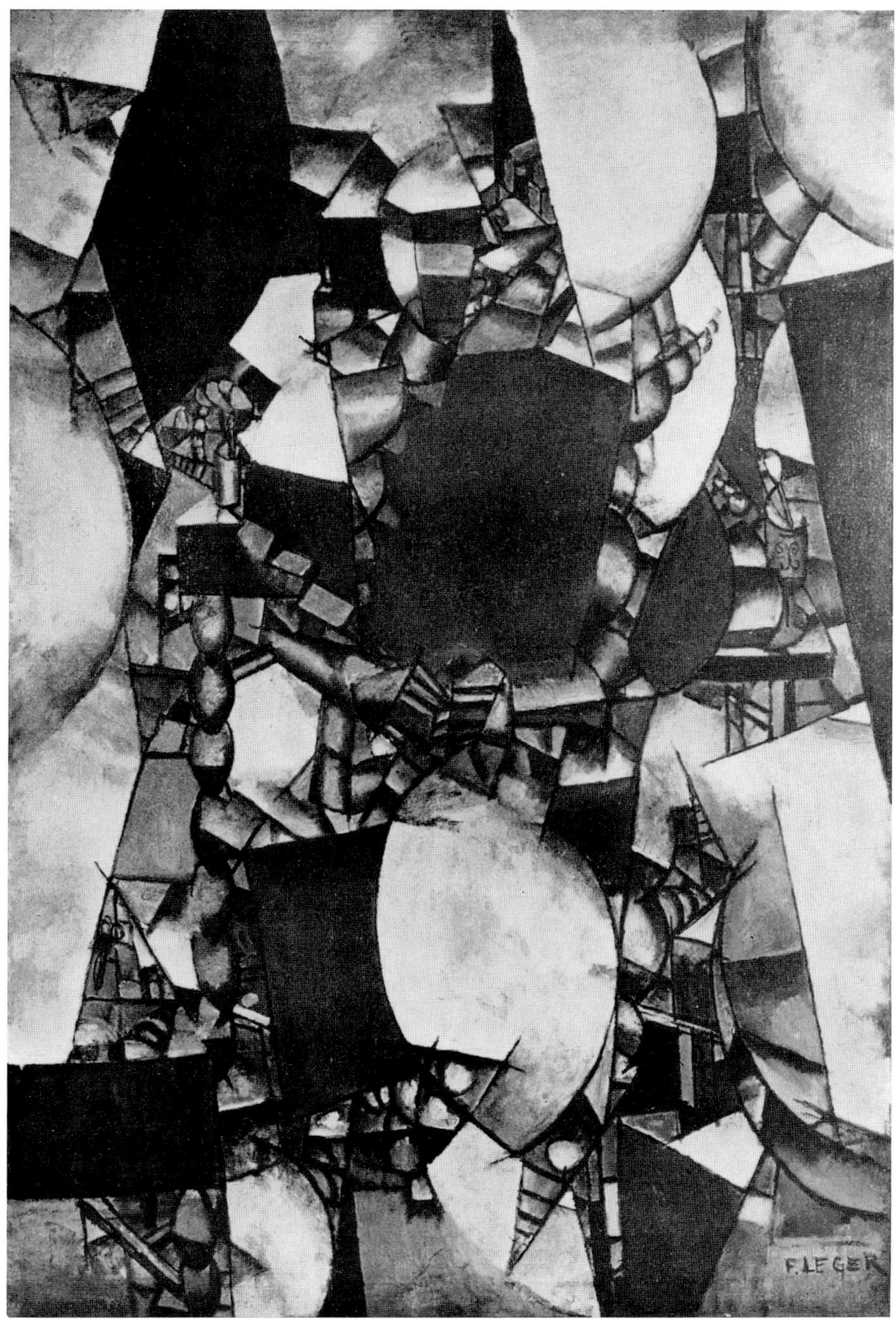

Fig. 20 FERNAND LÉGER   WOMAN IN BLUE.   1912

Second stage of Cubism. The verticality of the surface is more important than the receding volume. Léger is more concerned with the contrasts between straight and curved forms than with an analysis of the object that is dependent on different points of view. The description is reduced to supreme simplification, without being suspended entirely. The color is applied to the white priming of the canvas.

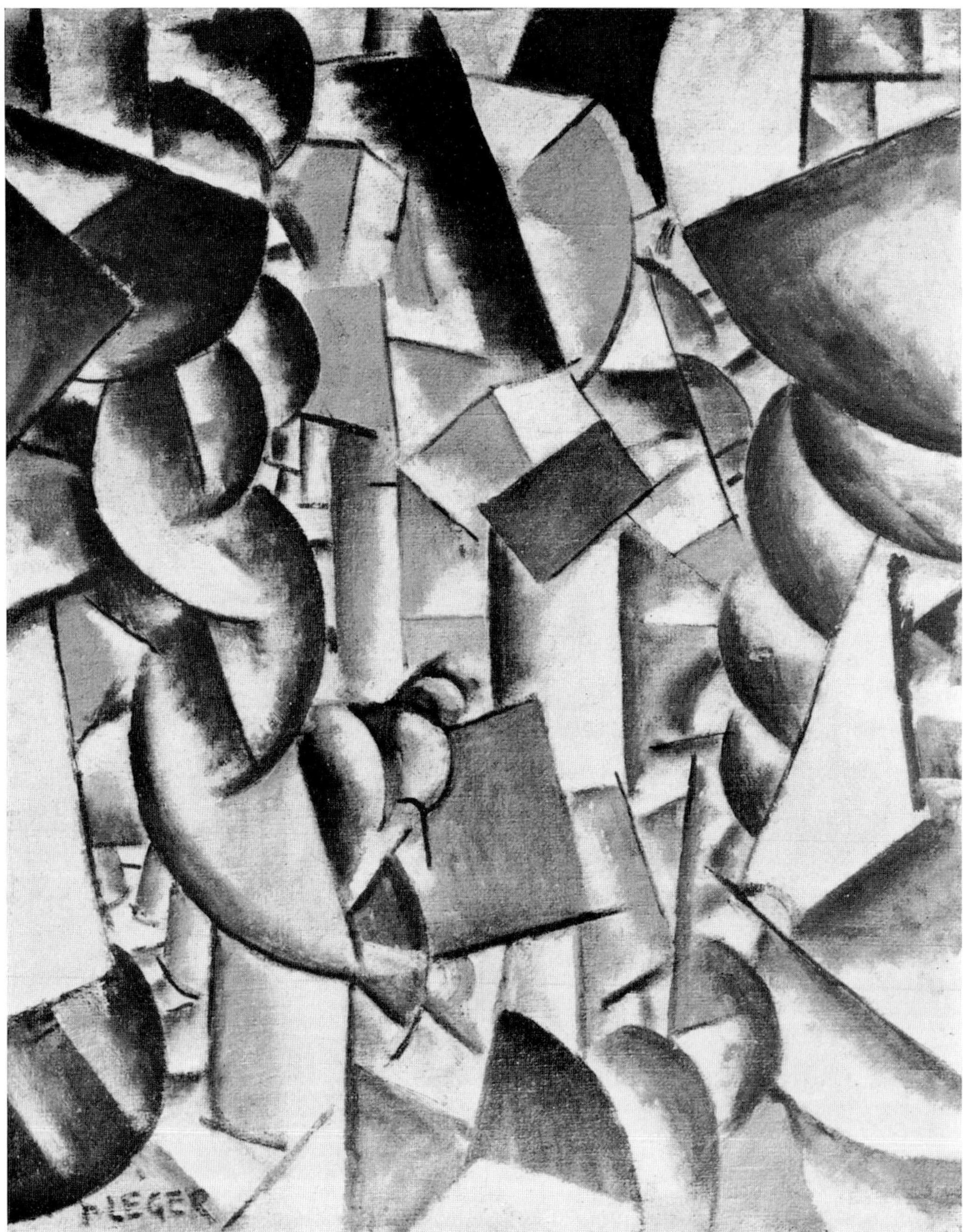

Fig. 21 FERNAND LÉGER   ROOFS IN THE FOREST.   1914.

A further example of the second stage of Cubism. The contrasts between straight and curving lines are becoming increasingly prominent. During this period, Léger speaks intuitively of his wish to realize an expression of dynamic composition: later he takes up Delaunay's rotating circles.

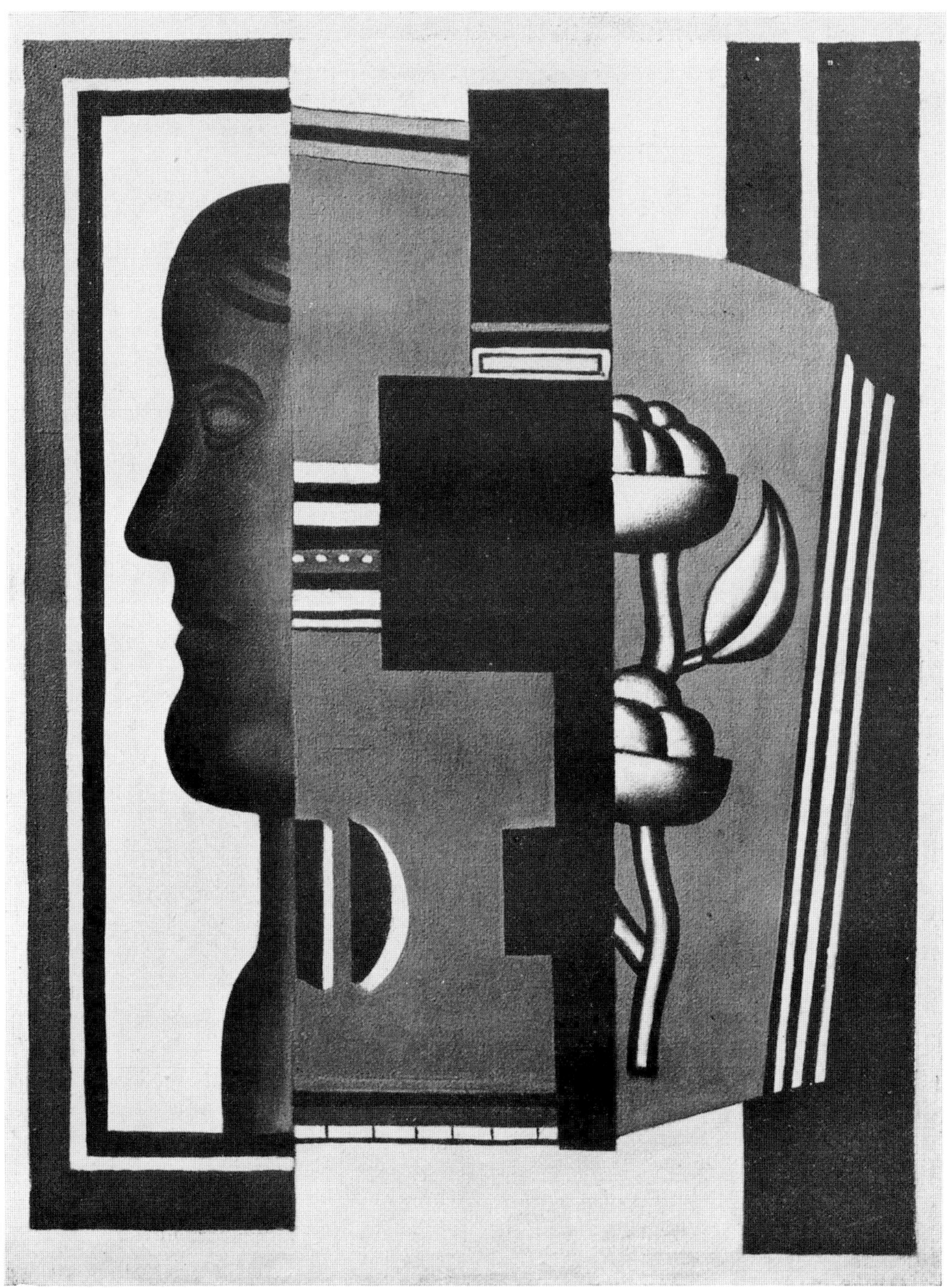

Third stage of Cubism. Here the nature of the flat plane wins against the artist's technique. Without completely dispensing with volume or description, but with contrast and distinction between two attitudes. Juxtaposition of the dogma of the Renaissance with its modeling and the composition of the Christian dogma with its circular planar form, which had exclusive validity until the thir=teenth century.

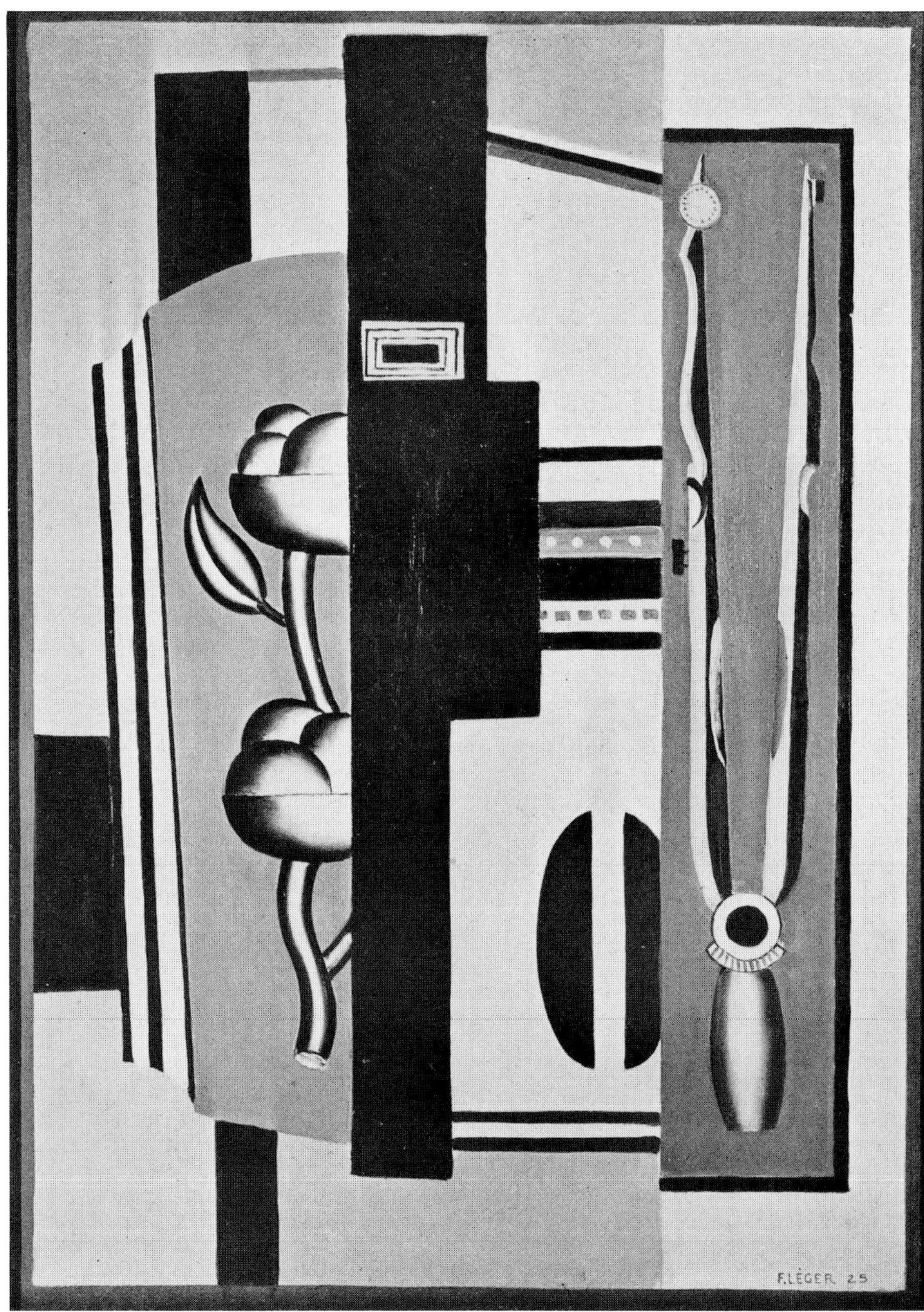

Fig. 23 FERNAND LÉGER FLOWERS AND COMPASS. 1925

Third stage of Cubism. The same as in the previous illustration.

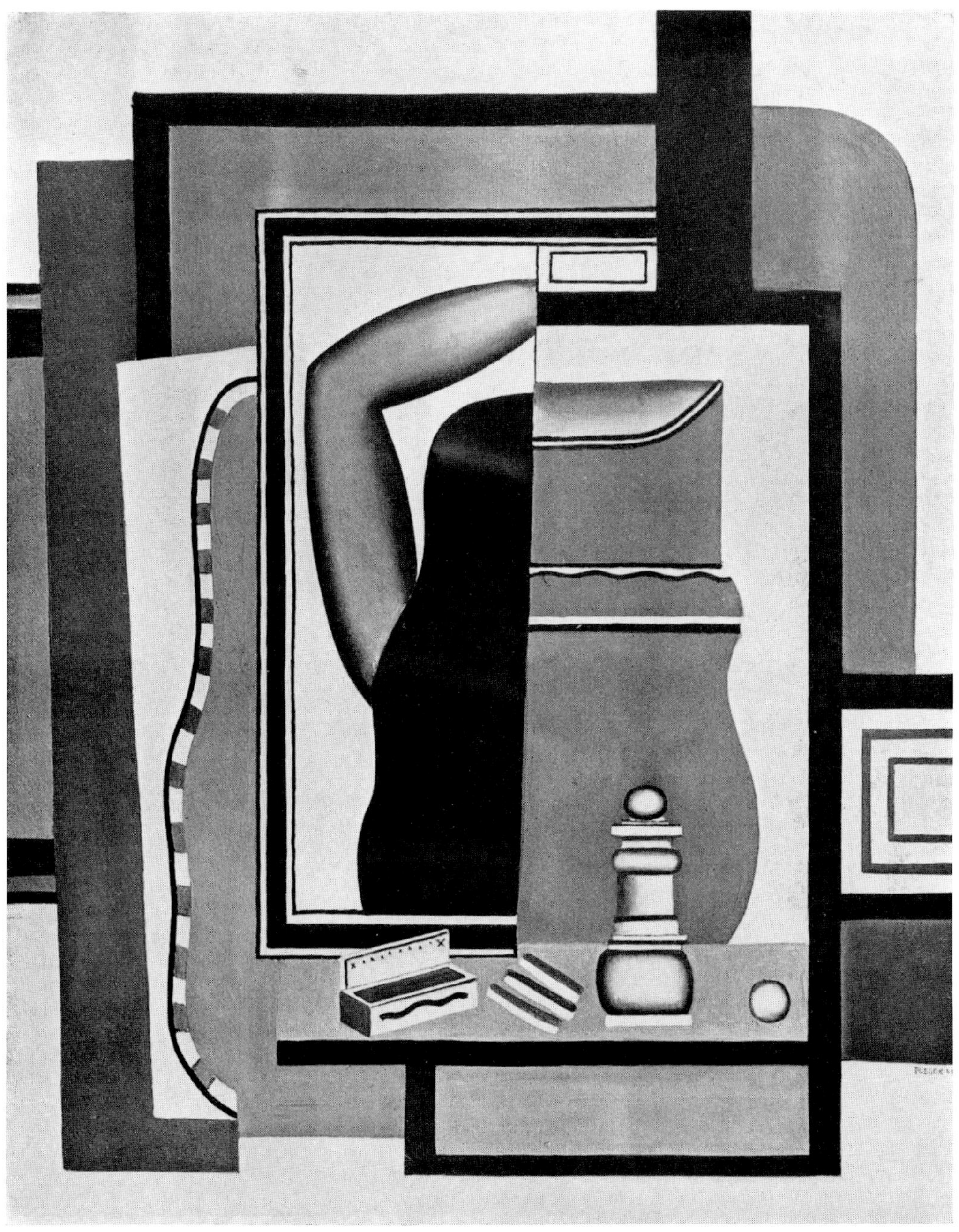

Fig. 24 FERNAND LÉGER WOMAN AT HER TOILET. 1925

Third stage of Cubism. Here the same applies as in Figs. 22 and 23. The plane is animated and subdivided, corresponding to the one aspect of its nature, the displacement. Its ability to rotate is not taken into consideration.

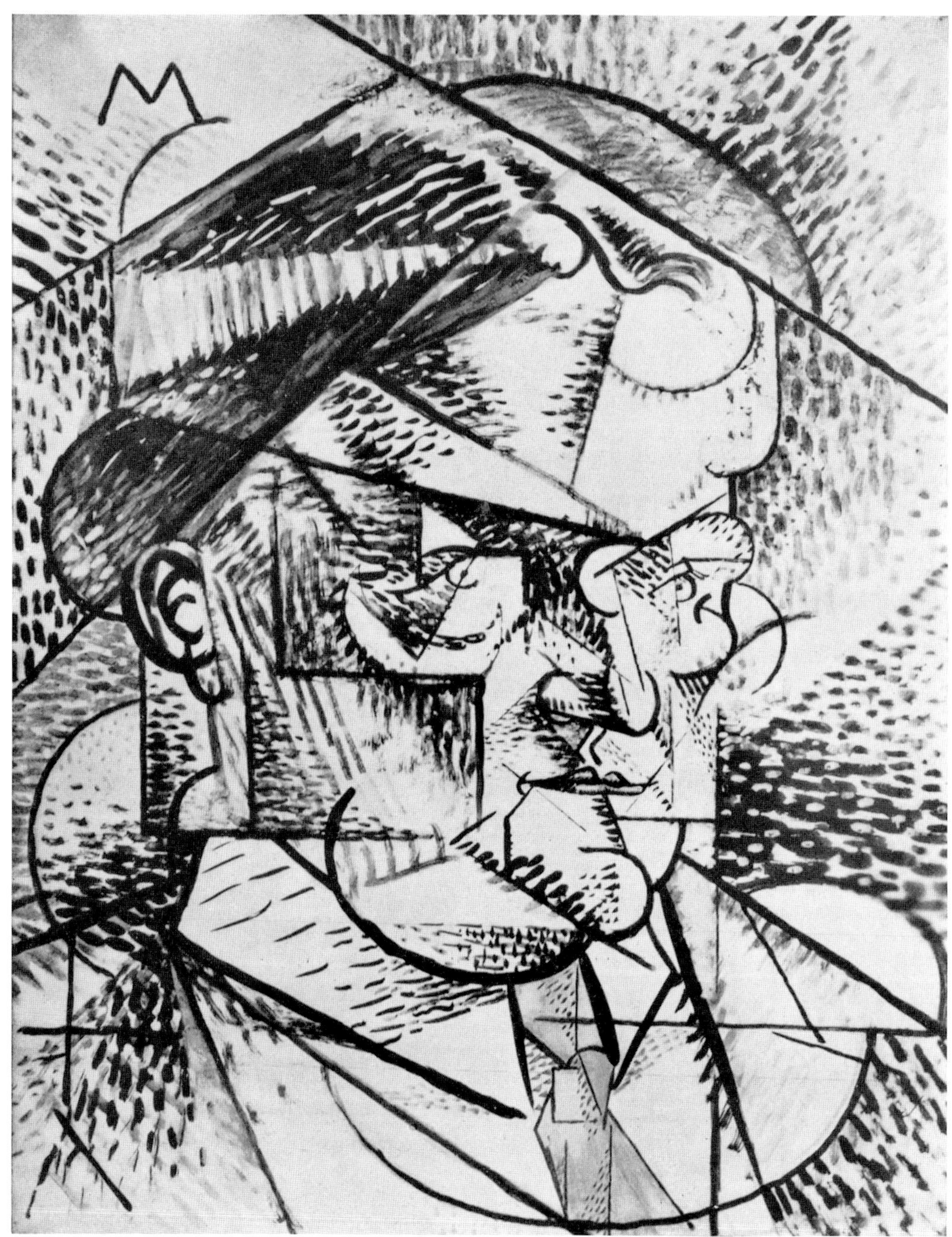

Fig. 25 LOUIS MARCOUSSIS PORTRAIT. 1912

Second stage of Cubism. Multiplicity of points of view. Volume governed by the plane. Description in fragments.

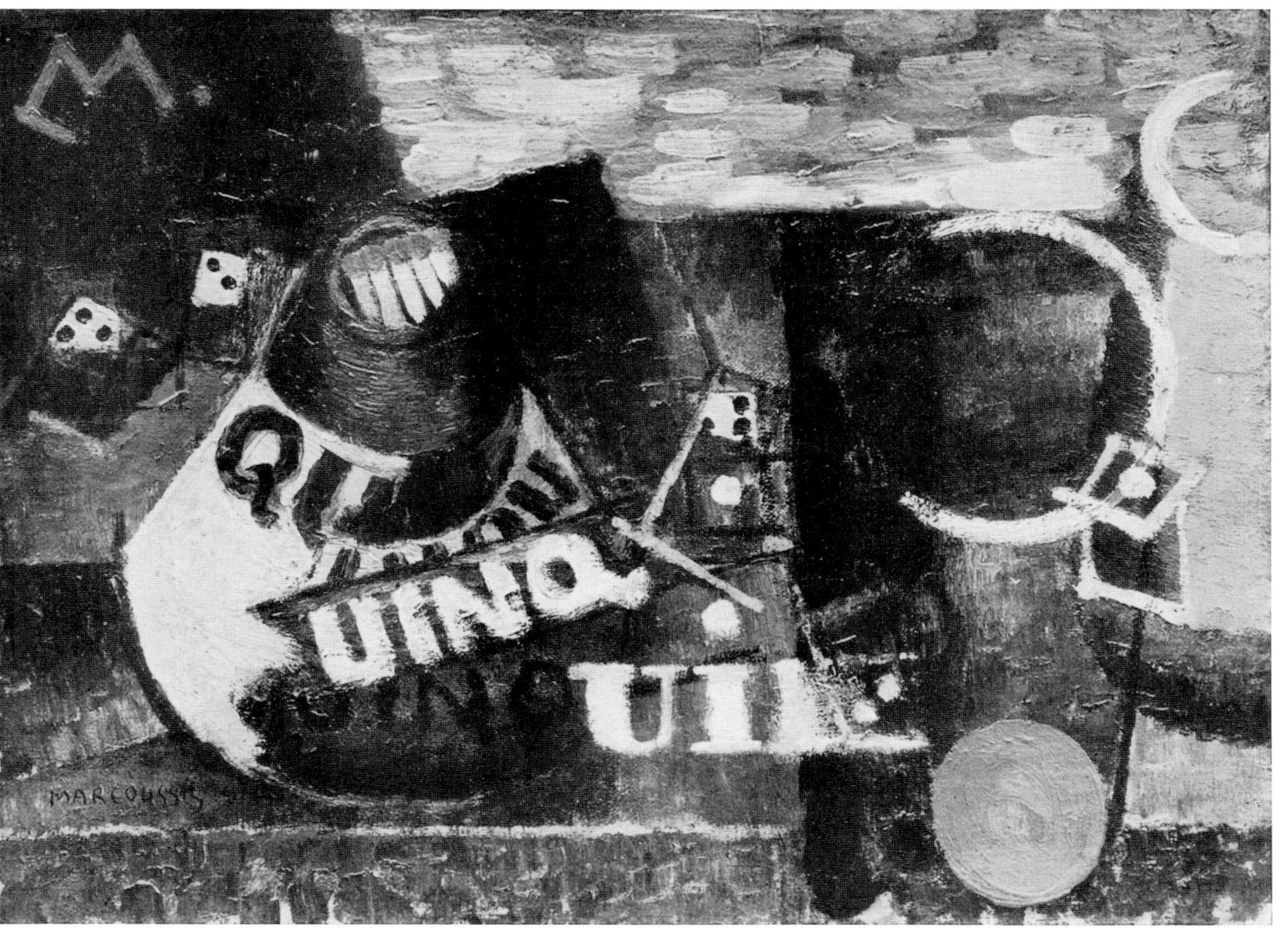

Fig. 26 LOUIS MARCOUSSIS VOLCANIC. 1914

Second stage of Cubism. The same as in the previous illustration. The plane presses forward in order take the lead in the composition. The description is concentrated.

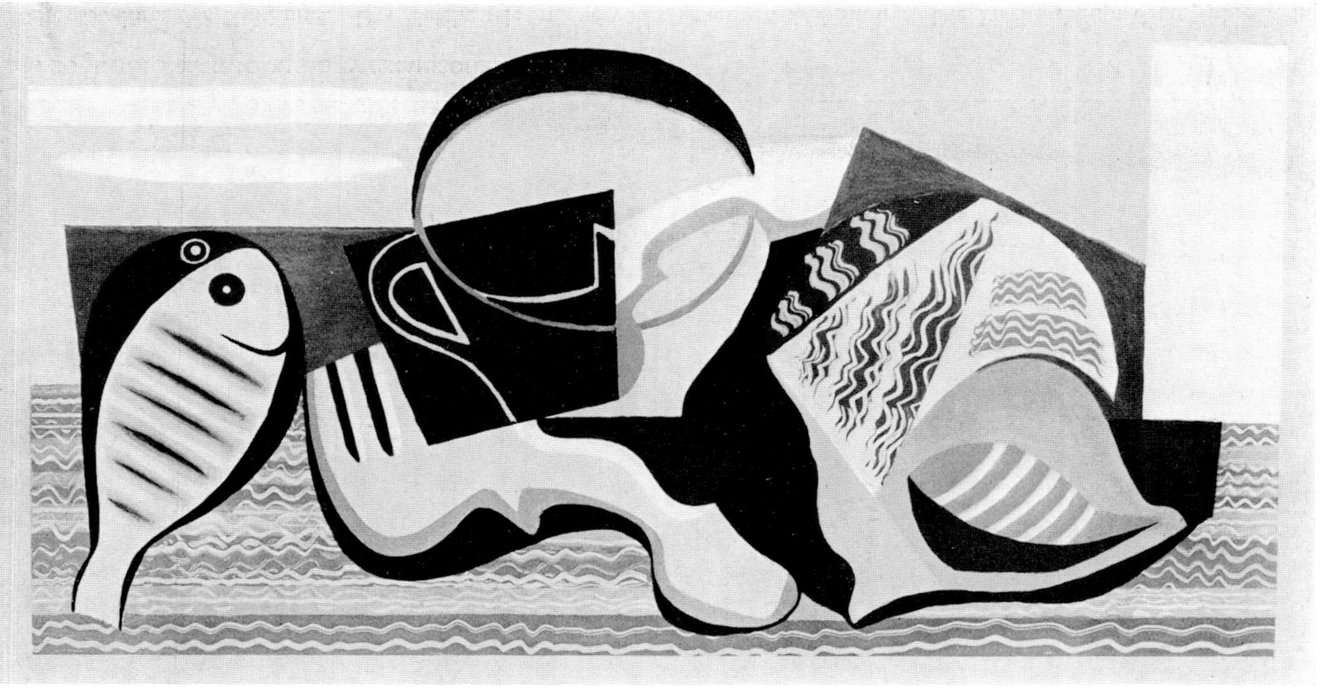

Fig. 27 LOUIS MARCOUSSIS STILL LIFE. 1926

Third stage of Cubism. Concentration on the descriptive pictorial elements, reduced to a scheme of their geometric dimensions. A rhythm attempts to connect their respective subcomponents. The various planes introduce movement into the static composition through their material contrasts.

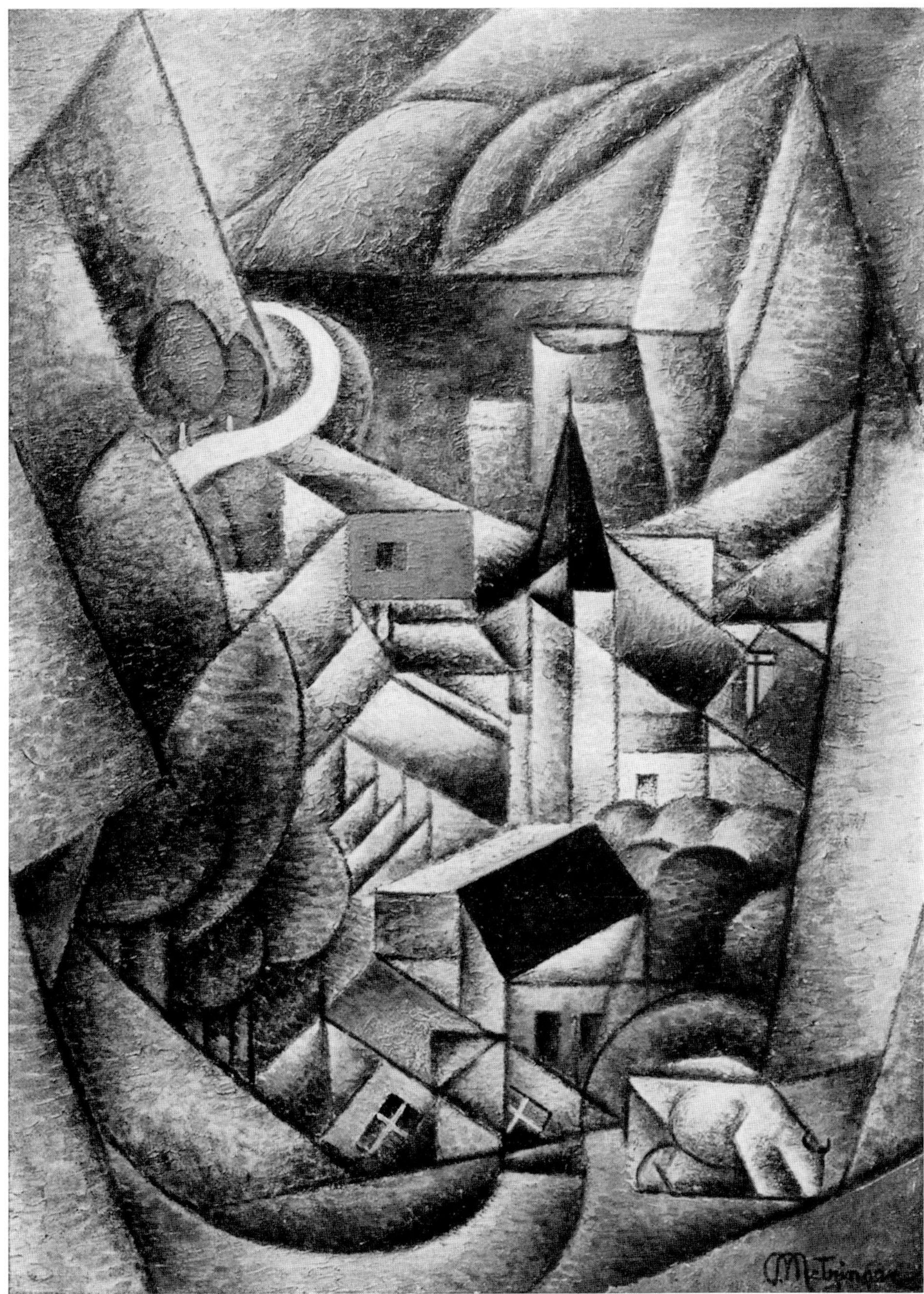

Fig. 28 JEAN METZINGER LANDSCAPE. 1911

First and second stage of Cubism. This picture, created in 1911, is one of the finest of this period. It not only makes promises, but offers fulfillment. Although the idea of volume is still adopted by the artist and the unifying and centralizing perspective is initially taken into account, we must nonetheless admit that these terms are already beginning to lose their significance through the importance of new goals. On this canvas, we sense the multiplicity of perspectival points of view, the supremacy of the plane, its ability to gain dynamic life through displacement and rotation, the rhythmical liaison and already the concentration of the composition within the boundaries of the picture. The paint application in particular creates an overall impression of colorful grays.

Second stage
of Cubism.
The same
comments as
for the previ=
ous painting.
What an in=
tellectual rev=
olution in
this destruc=
tion of Re=
naissance de=
scription!

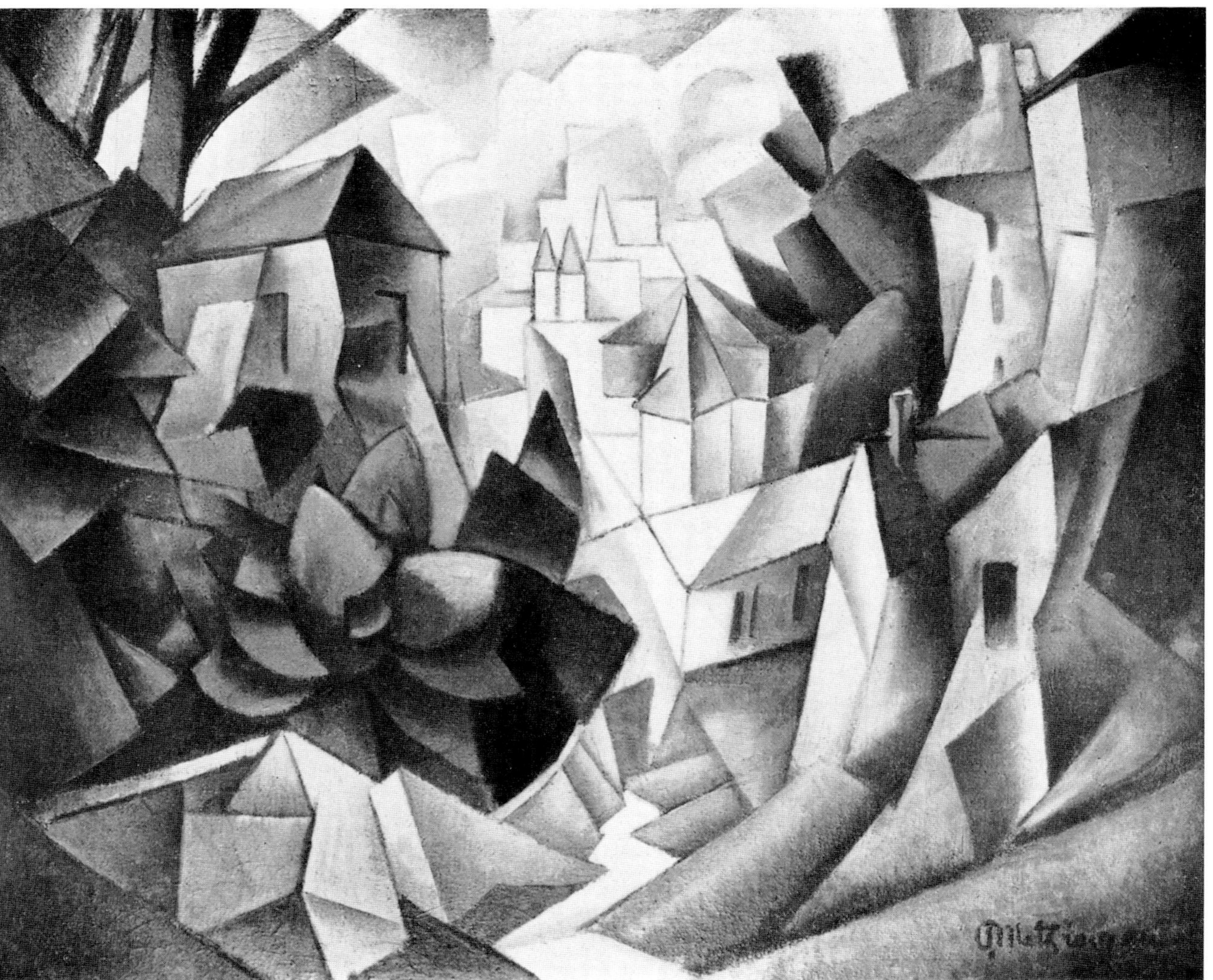

Fig. 29 JEAN METZINGER LANDSCAPE. 1912

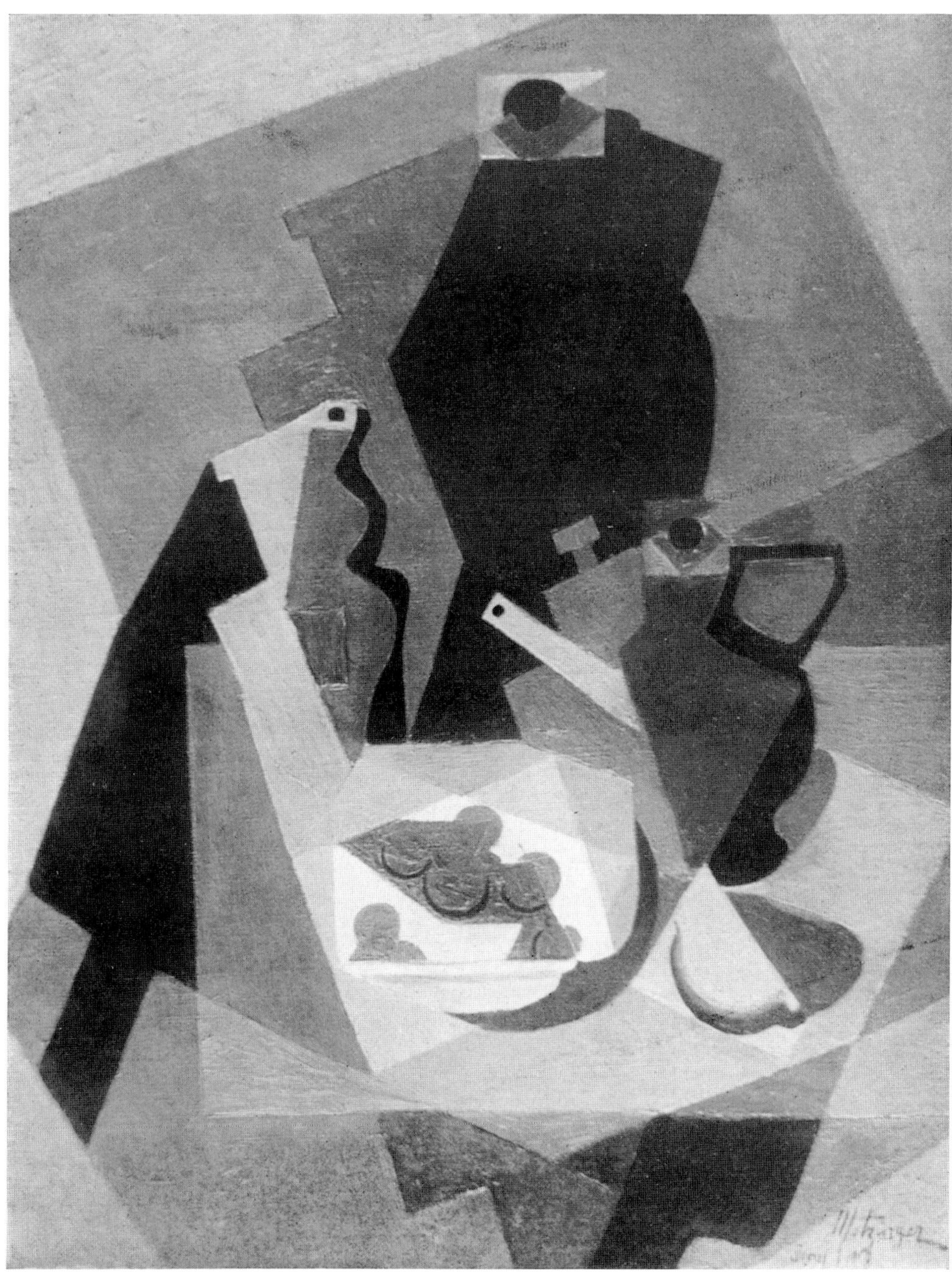

Fig. 30 JEAN METZINGER STILL LIFE. 1917

Third stage of Cubism. The convulsion calms down. The volume has disappeared together with the naive description. With the renewed sentiment, a new order rises. The plane gains life of its own accord, corresponding to its nature. The t e m p o r a l f o r m makes an appearance, circling, cohesive, arising from the d i s p l a c e m e n t — a compositional solution to the geometric perspective which is hostile to form — and from the r o t a t i o n — a compositional solution from the principles of the compositional structure — held together in its sensuous phases by an intellectual rhythm.

First and second stages of Cubism. Hitherto, Picasso has progressed through the stage of pure volume. Here, too, there is still an adhering to the idea of sche=matized volume, which exists alongside other aims; therefore, simultaneously, the multiplicity of points of view and the paramount importance of the plane. In my opin=ion, the letters mean the intro=duction of an ele=ment of great boldness and min=imal intellectuali=ty into the Renais=sance=style paint=ing. They renew the simple and di=rect technique of the mural painter, the sign writer, the decorative crafts=man, in contrast to the complicated and outward show of the artist.

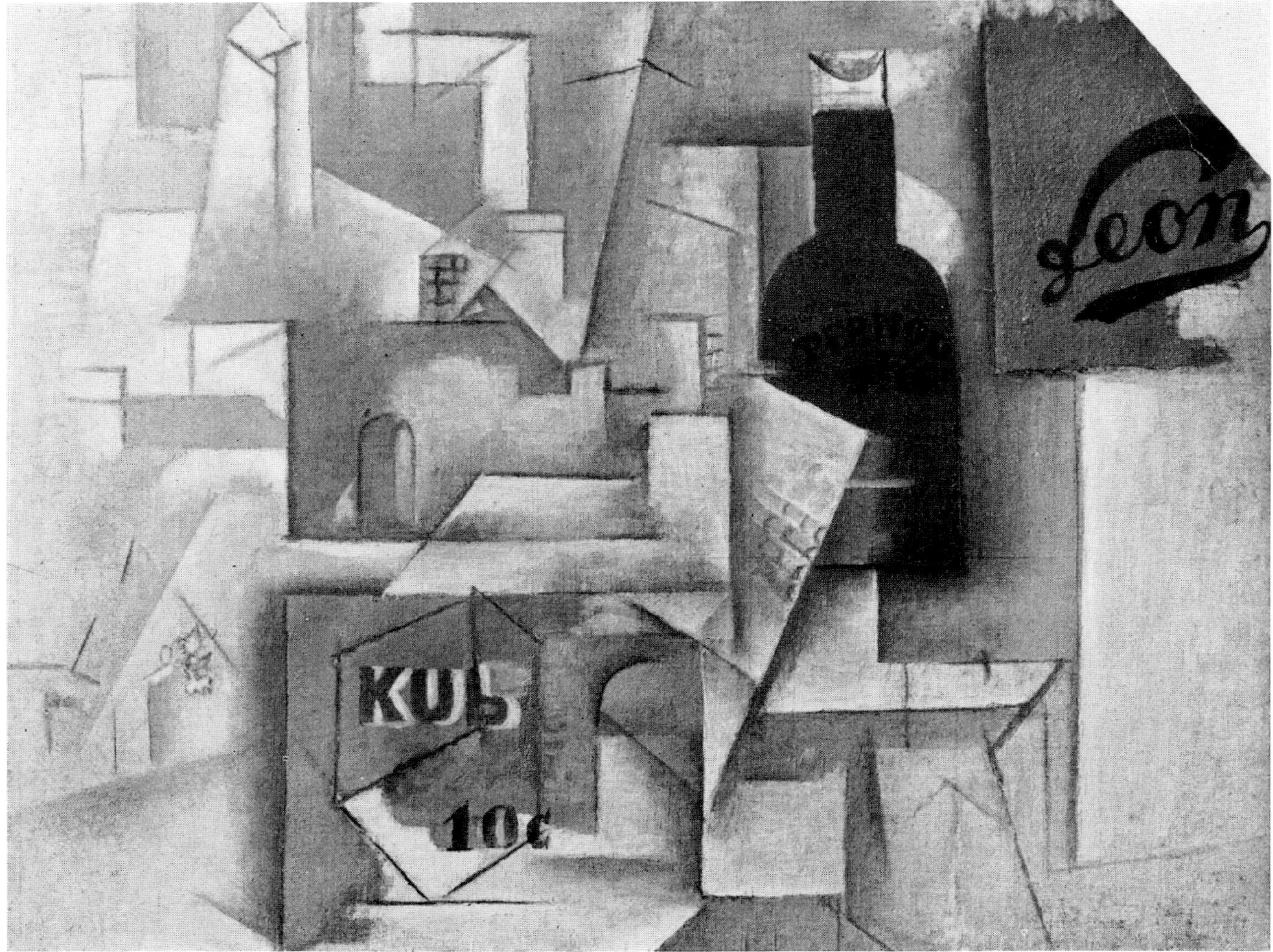

Fig. 31 PABLO PICASSO VIEW OF AVIGNON. 1913

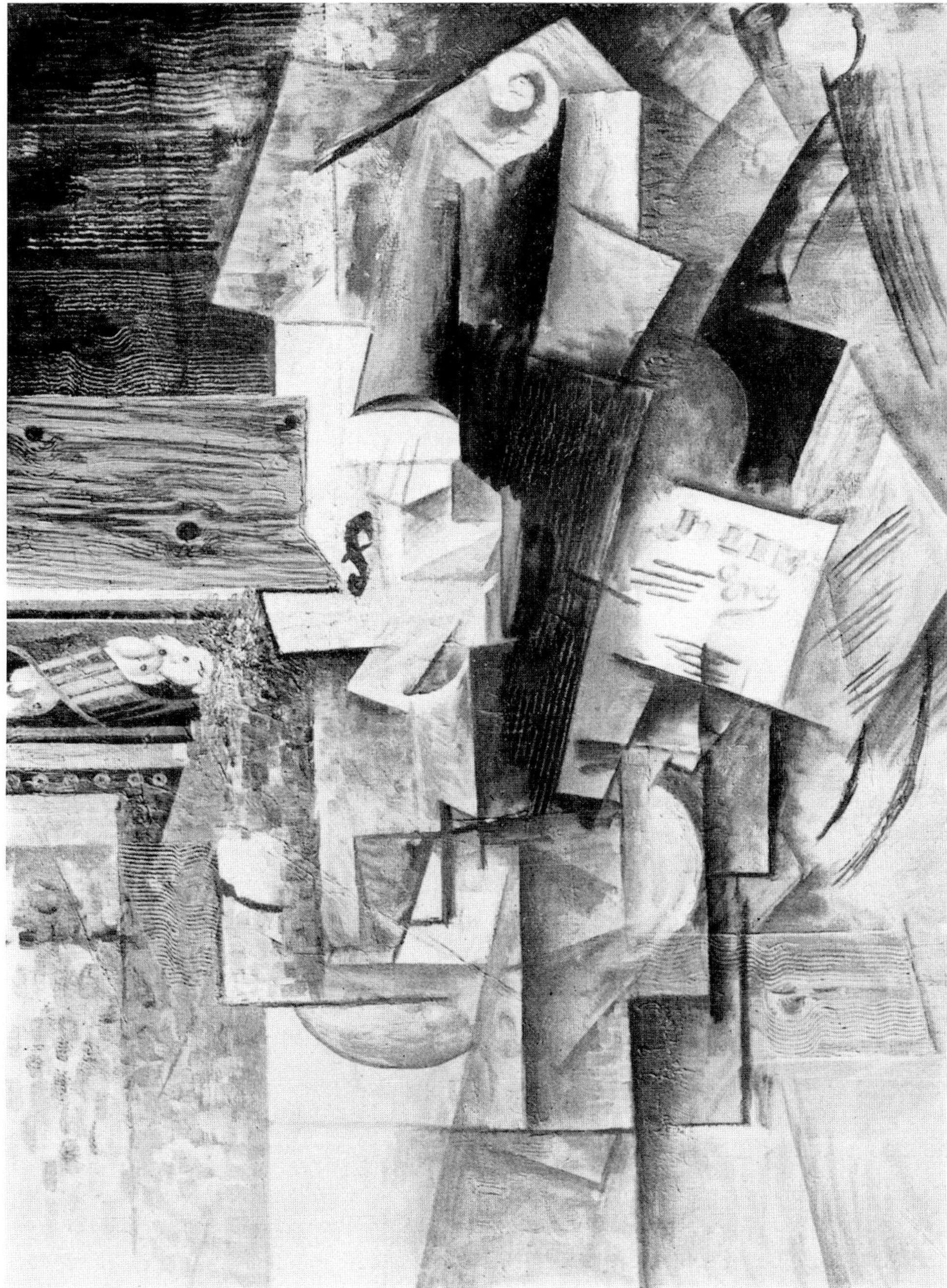

Fig. 32 PABLO PICASSO VIOLIN. 1913

Second stage of Cubism, which is expressed in this example in great purity. The volume has completely disappeared. The descriptive is simply a listing of geometric extensions. The directions of the pictorial elements selected by the artist follow the natural directions of the plane. The material multiplicity underlines increasingly the technique of the mural painter: a wall painting with the particular characteristic and permanence of its means in contrast to painting on an easel, whose principles will not be shaken when the generally accepted term of description makes such astounding advances into the area of a private metaphysics. Here the boldness lies more in these craftsmanlike borrowings, these attributes of the workshop, which damage the respectability of the artistic painting, than in the narrative incomprehensibility of the object.

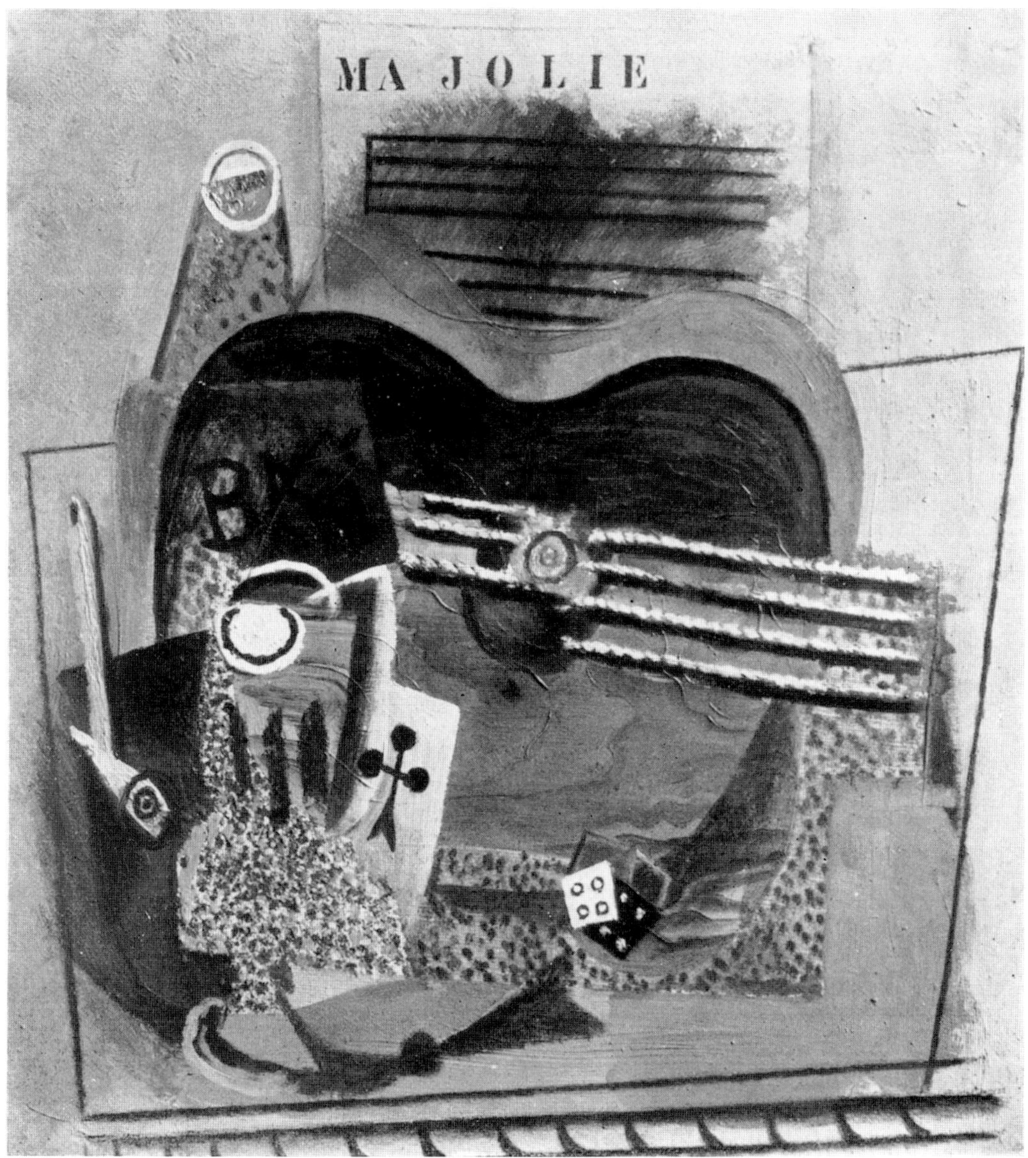

Fig. 33 PABLO PICASSO STILL LIFE. 1914

Third stage of Cubism. The compositional credibility of the vertical plane is even greater. The composition therefore has become simpler, purer, more expressive. — Picasso possesses a remarkable instinct, but reveals less logic of conscience and wisdom than Gris and Metzinger. That is his irresistible charm, his particular attraction for a public that is besotted with the conventional, one that forgives the artist these technical lapses. Grew up in love and respect for the old masters and museums. There is evidence of this in his entire significant oeuvre. And that is the reason why his work is divided into two parts: descriptive painting (to a certain extent the result of his first training) and invented, creative works (the product of his own temperament). But his individual case preys on his mind. In the works of Gris and Metzinger, more new discoveries. Their influence, their skill is less; their radiance, even in weaker works, is greater than that of Picasso. The future, unencumbered by the errors of today, will prove it: young artists will learn from them.

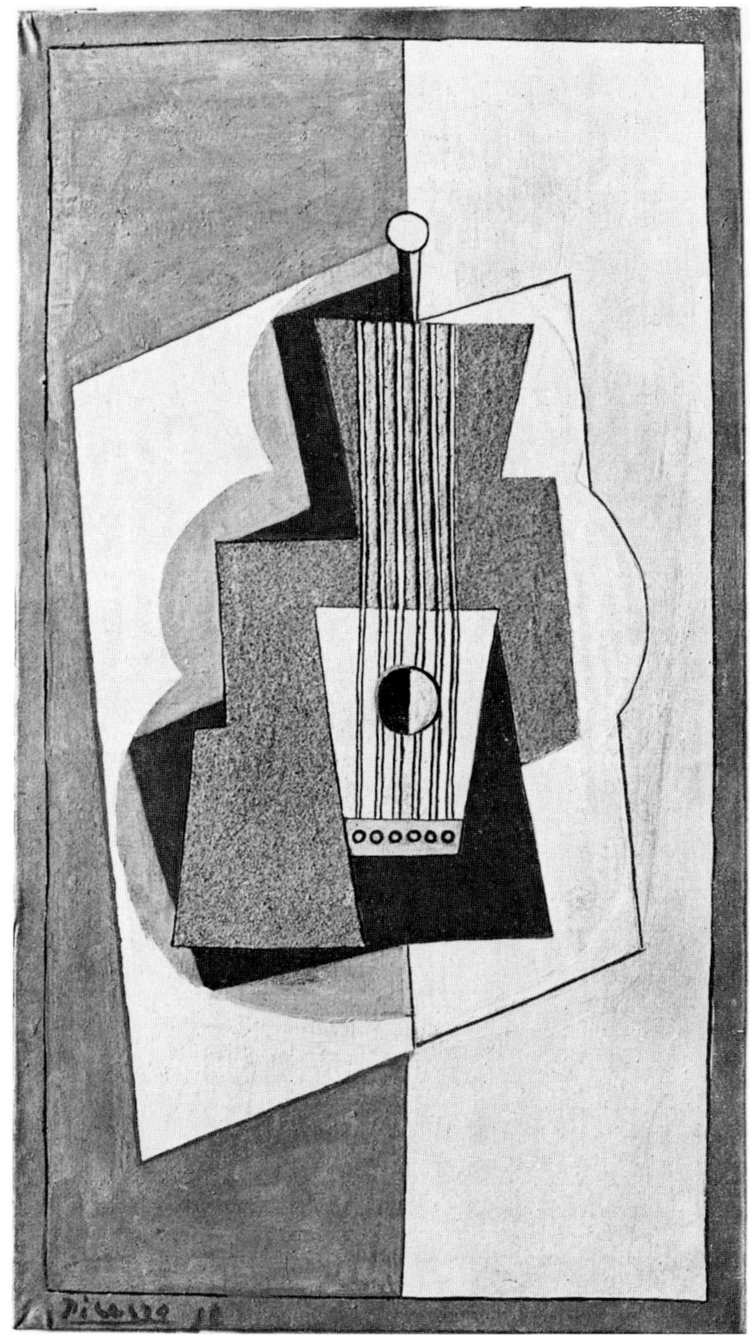

Fig. 34 PABLO PICASSO STILL LIFE (MUSIC). 1920

Third stage of Cubism. Greater purity and clarity. The compositional life of the plane would come closer to its realization if the painter as craftsman were to finally prevail over the "artist."

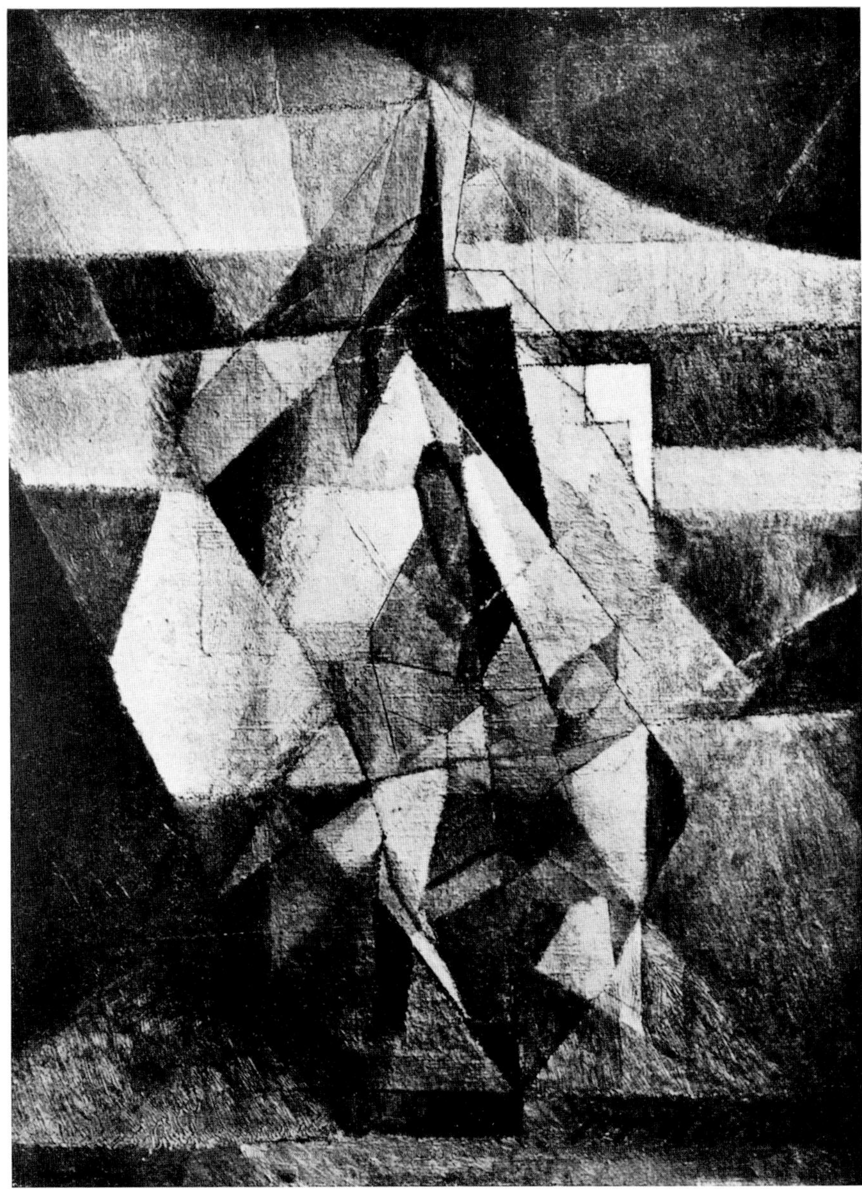

Fig. 35 JACQUES VILLON ROPE DANCER. 1913

Second stage of Cubism. Flatness, multiplicity of perspectival points of view.

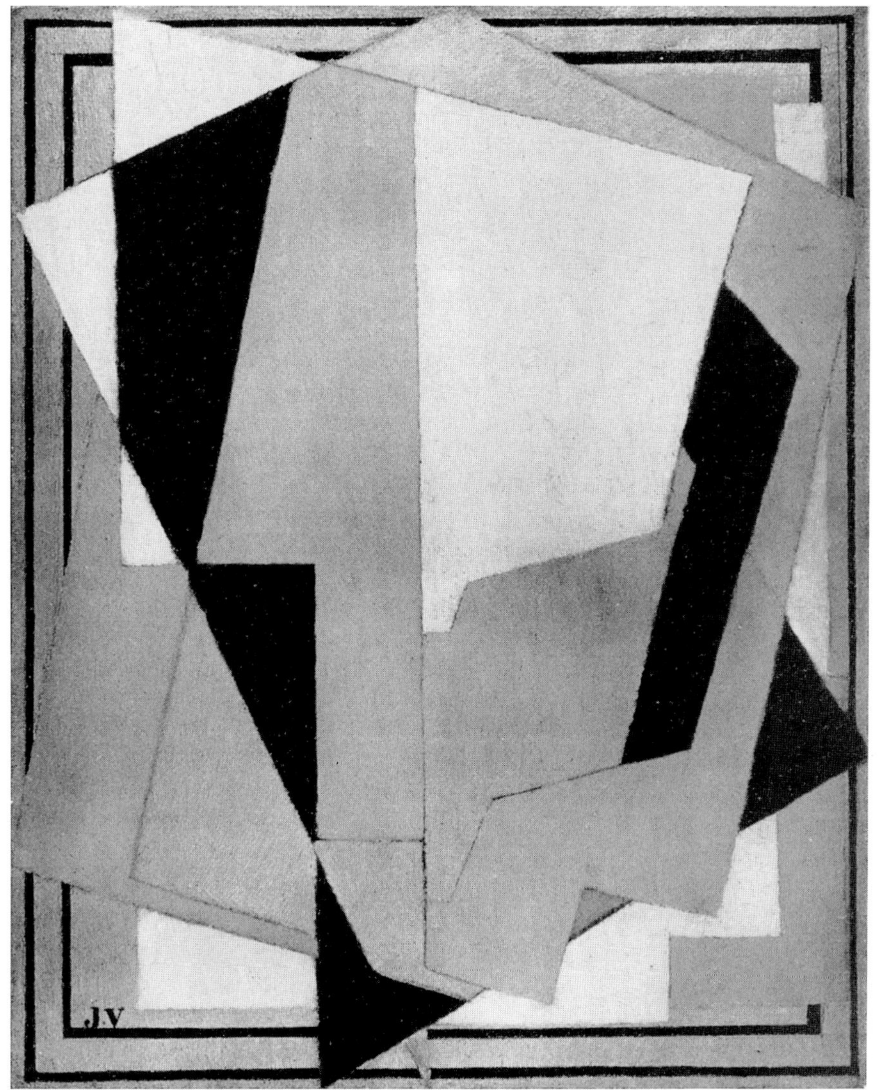

Fig. 36 JACQUES VILLON PAINTING. 1921

Third stage of Cubism. Scheme of the new design concept controlled by time. The plane has become flexible by means of displacement and rotation.

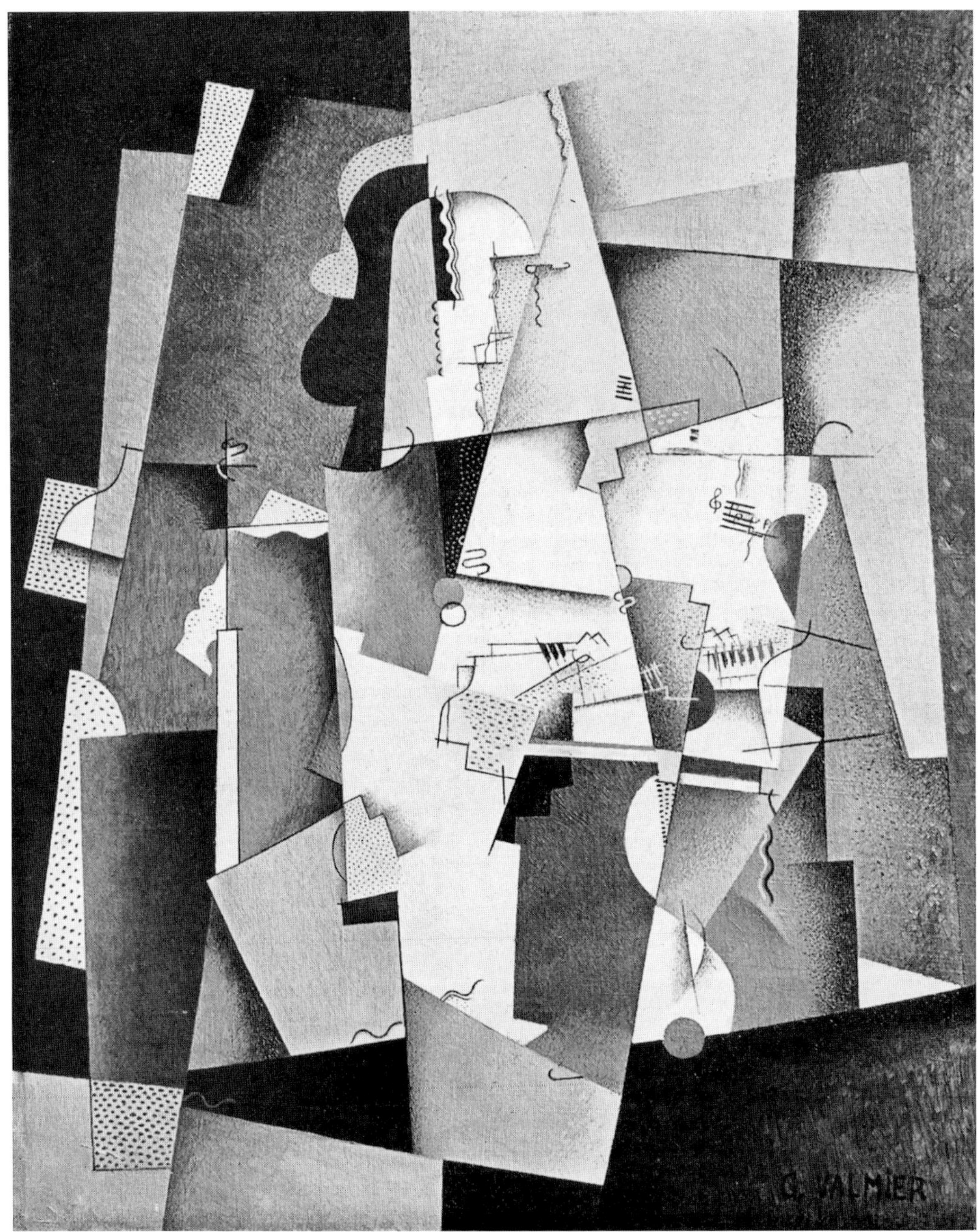

Fig. 37 GEORGES VALMIER FIGURE AT THE PIANO. 1920

Third stage of Cubism. The picture is a function of the plane.

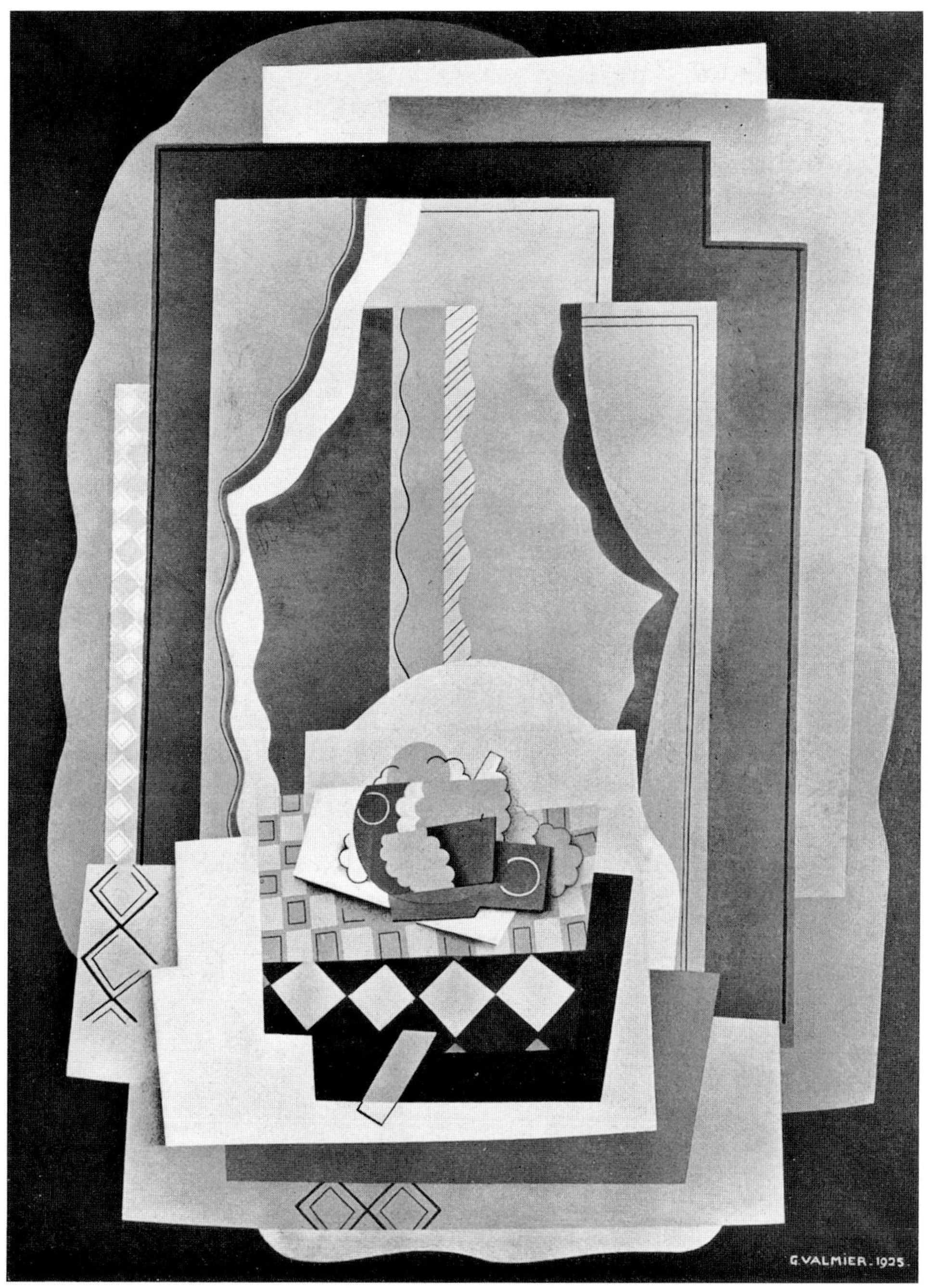

Fig. 38 GEORGES VALMIER STILL LIFE BY THE WINDOW. 1925

Third stage of Cubism. Rhythmic and compositional organization, corresponding to the nature of the plane.

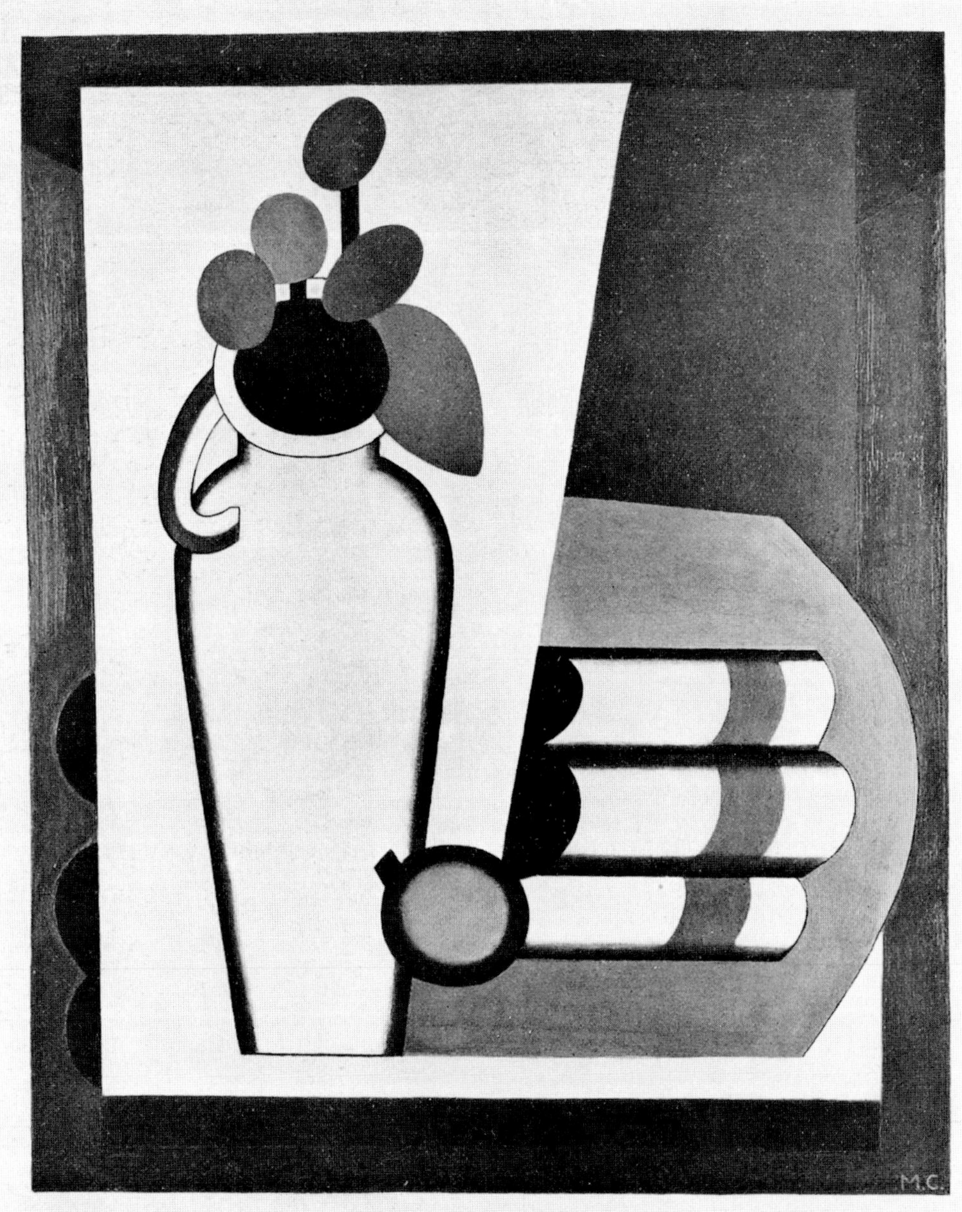

Fig. 39 MARCELLE CAHN STILL LIFE. 1925

Third stage of Cubism. The importance of the plane is recognized: by comparison the idea of the volume is dismantled and emphasizes the opposite for description by means of a hint of modeling. The plane moves only through displacement.

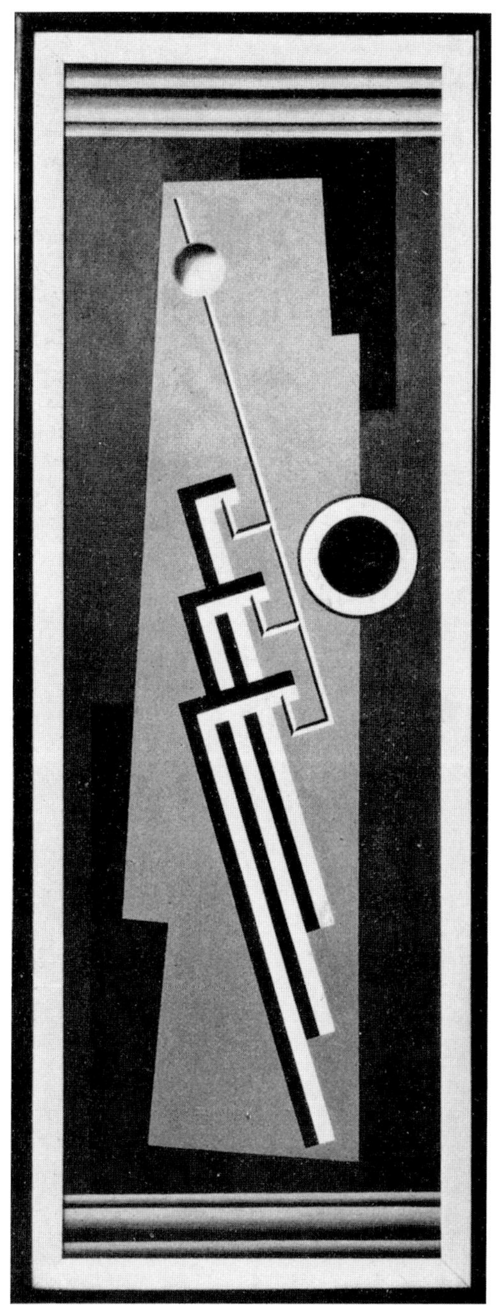

Third stage of Cubism. The same comments as for Fig. 39; striving for a more planar composition; the emphasis on the modeling weakens the rhythmic realization because the depth is accomplished for this very reason.

Fig. 40 OTTO CARLSUND WALL PAINTING. 1925

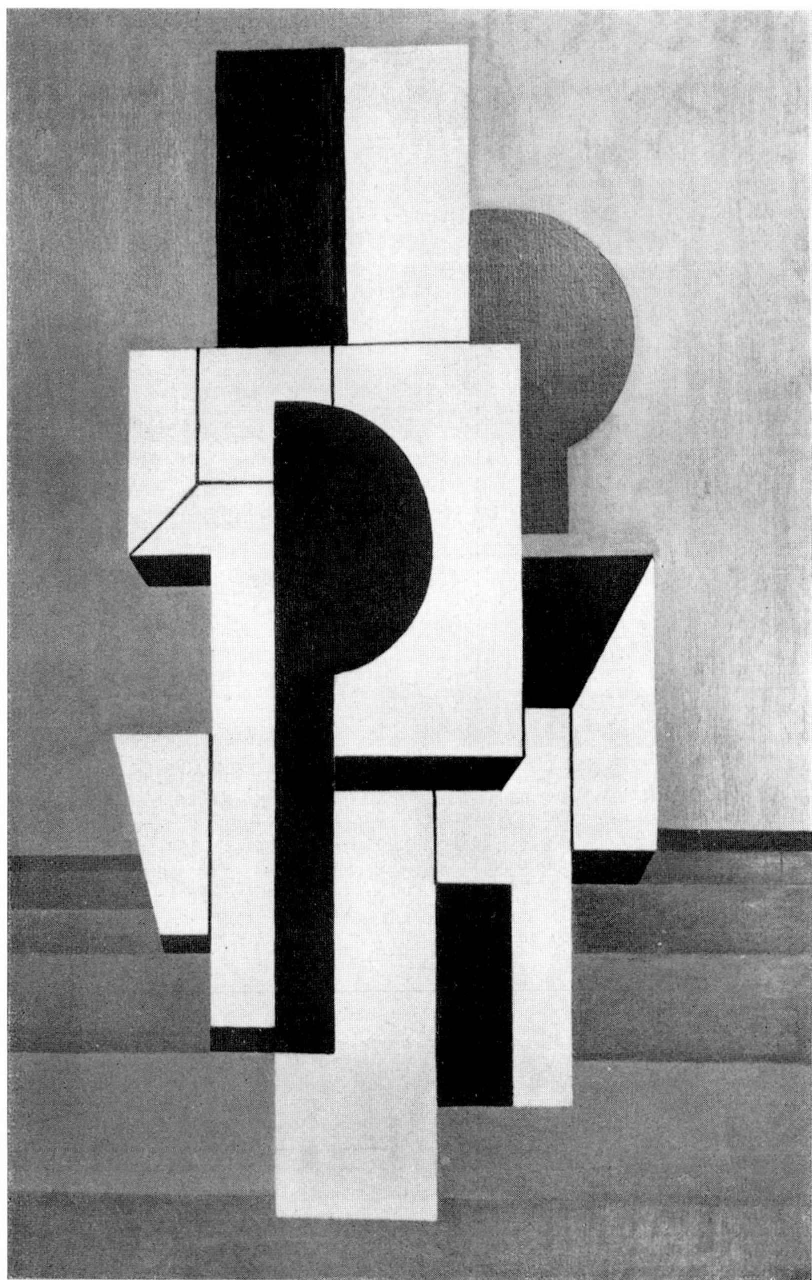

Third stage of Cubism. The same as before. The plane is in motion through the displacement.

Third stage of Cubism. The plane is acknowledged. The idea of description is still present, but only as a schematic representation of the analysis of the external views. Therefore the circumstance of the composition is already tangible. Intuitive application of the two preconditions for the flexible form: displacement and rotation.

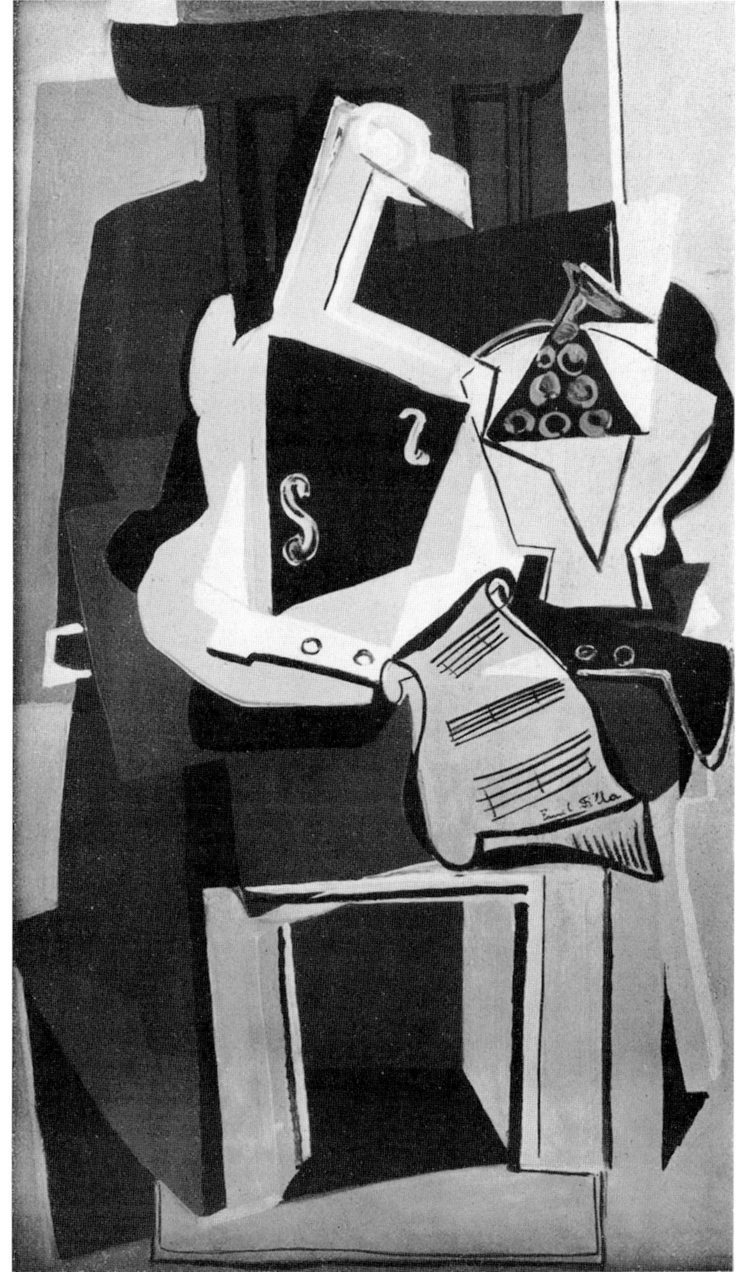

Fig. 42 EMIL FILLA STILL LIFE. 1925

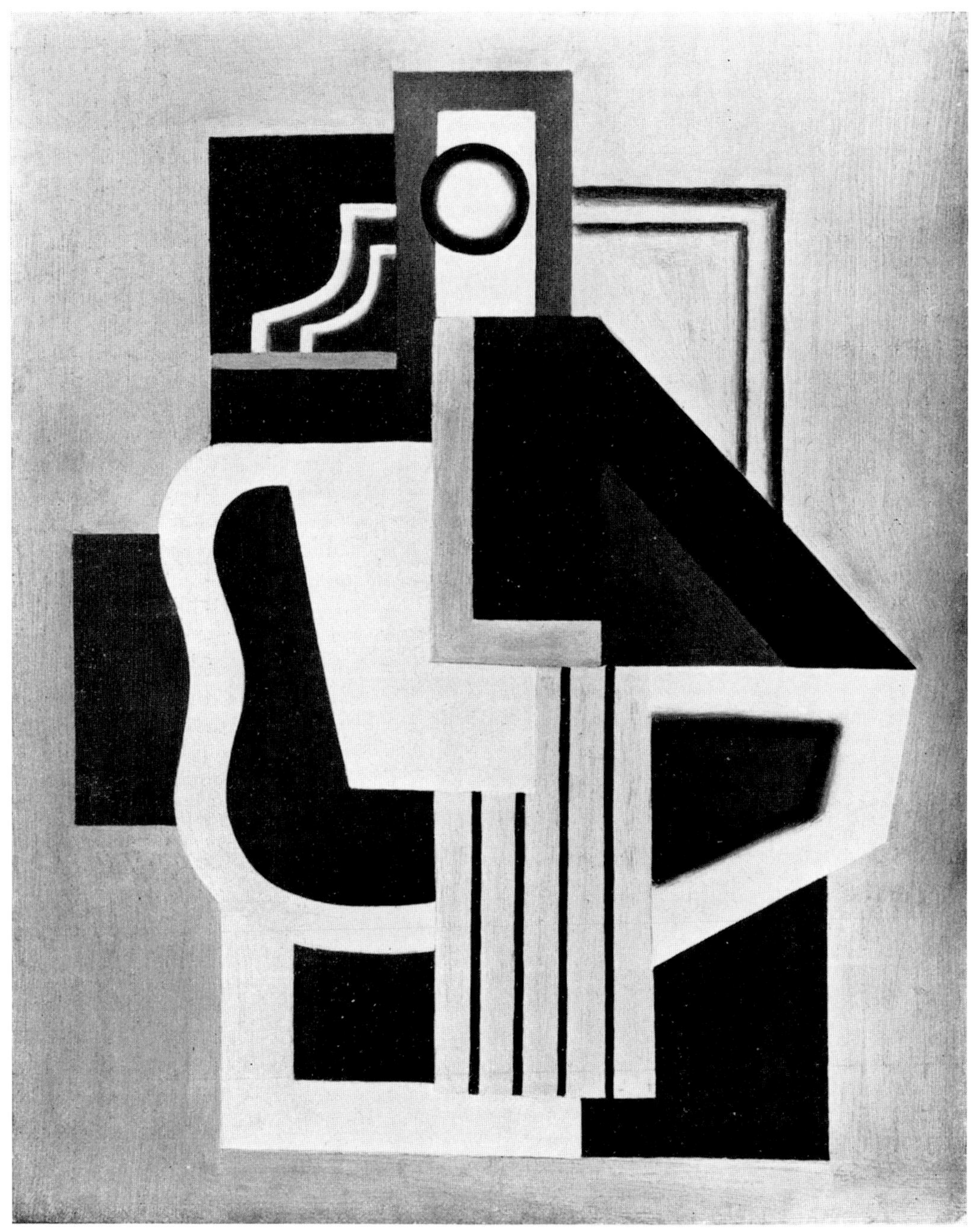

Fig. 43 FLORENCE HENRI COMPOSITION. 1926

Third stage of Cubism. Here the organization of the surface is clearer than in Fig. 42. A rhythm arises corresponding to the shift of the surface.

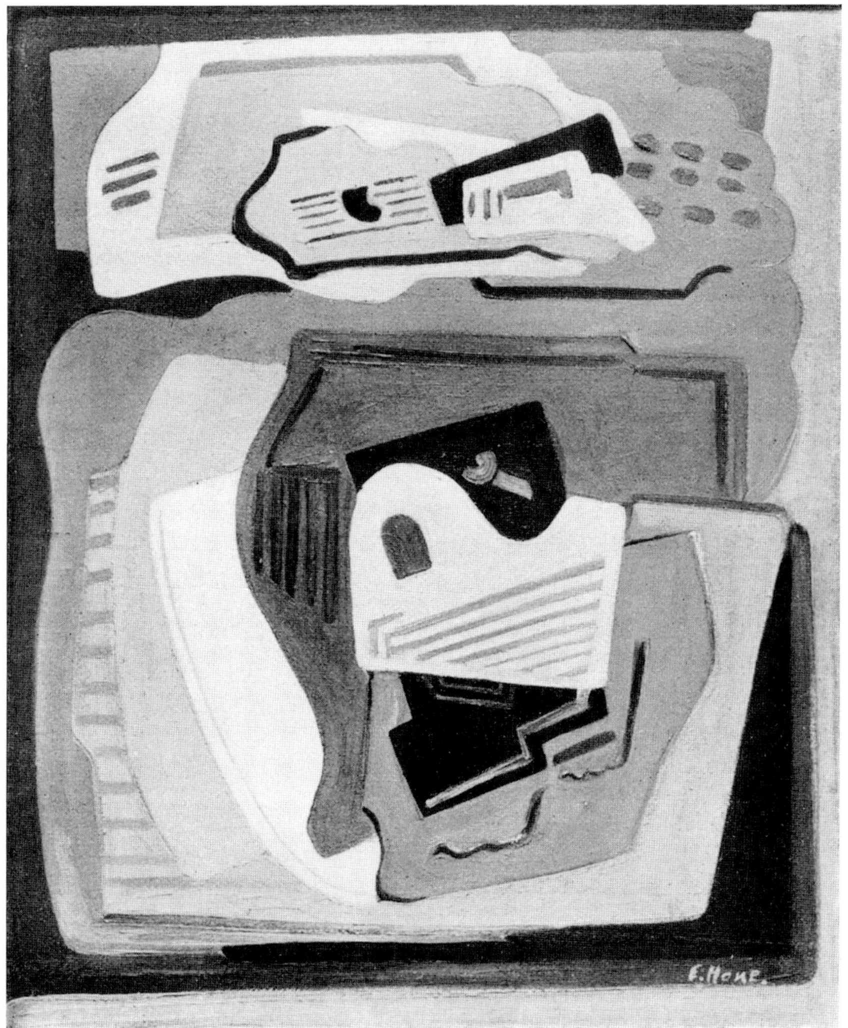

Fig. 44 E. HONE COMPOSITION IN TWO BASIC FORMS. 1925

Third stage of Cubism. The organization is composed architecturally: contrary to the large wall painting; albeit still on the individual level, but with the promise of monumental growth. A field of flowers is only a multiplication of flowers which are all co-ordinated; a tree is not an enlarged leaf. Monumental painting is not an element that has been increased beyond measure, but a multiplication of elements which normally belong together. Here the movement of the surface is through displacement and rotation.

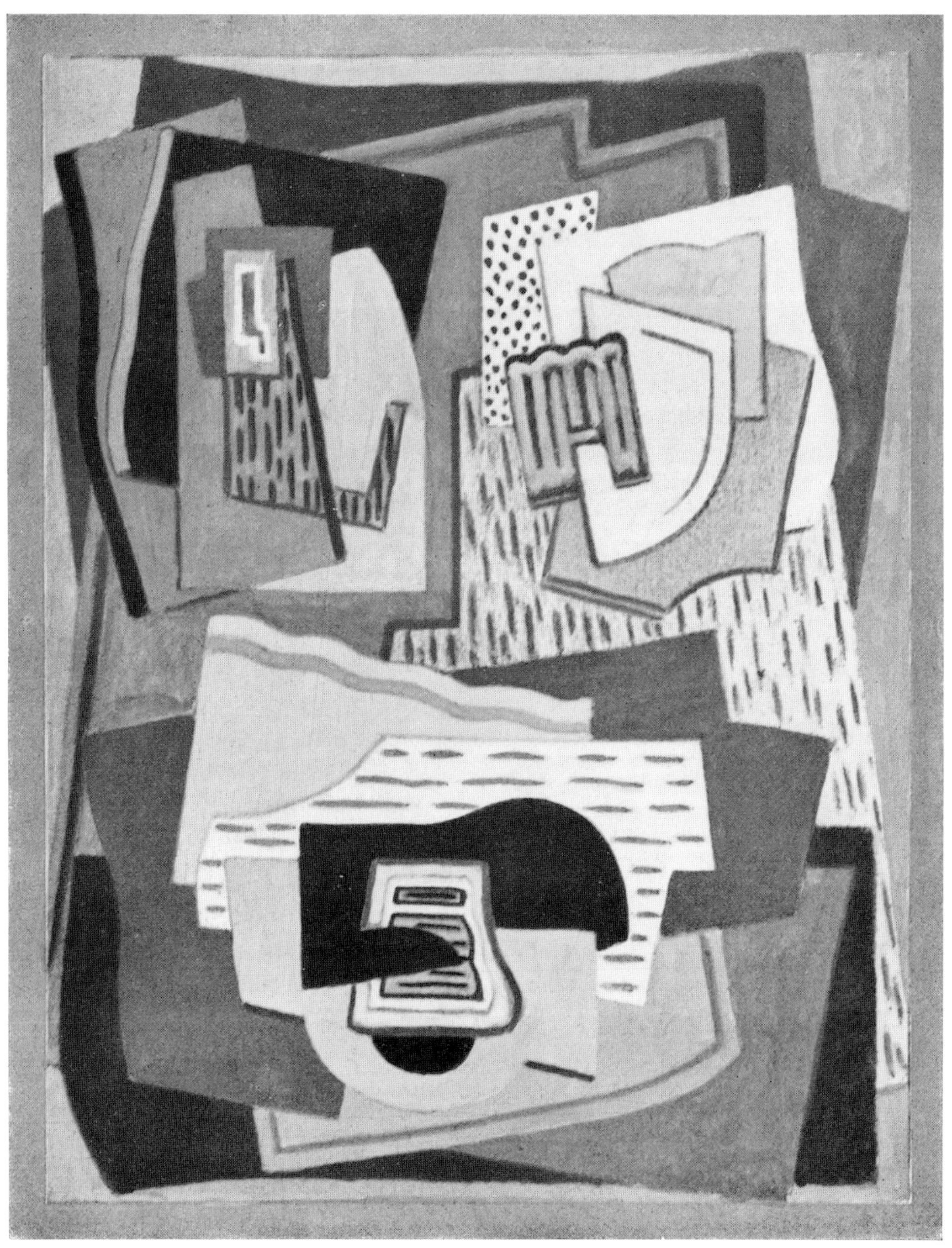

Fig. 45 M. JELLETT COMPOSITION IN THREE BASIC FORMS. 1925

Third stage of Cubism. Here the same applies as for Fig. 44.

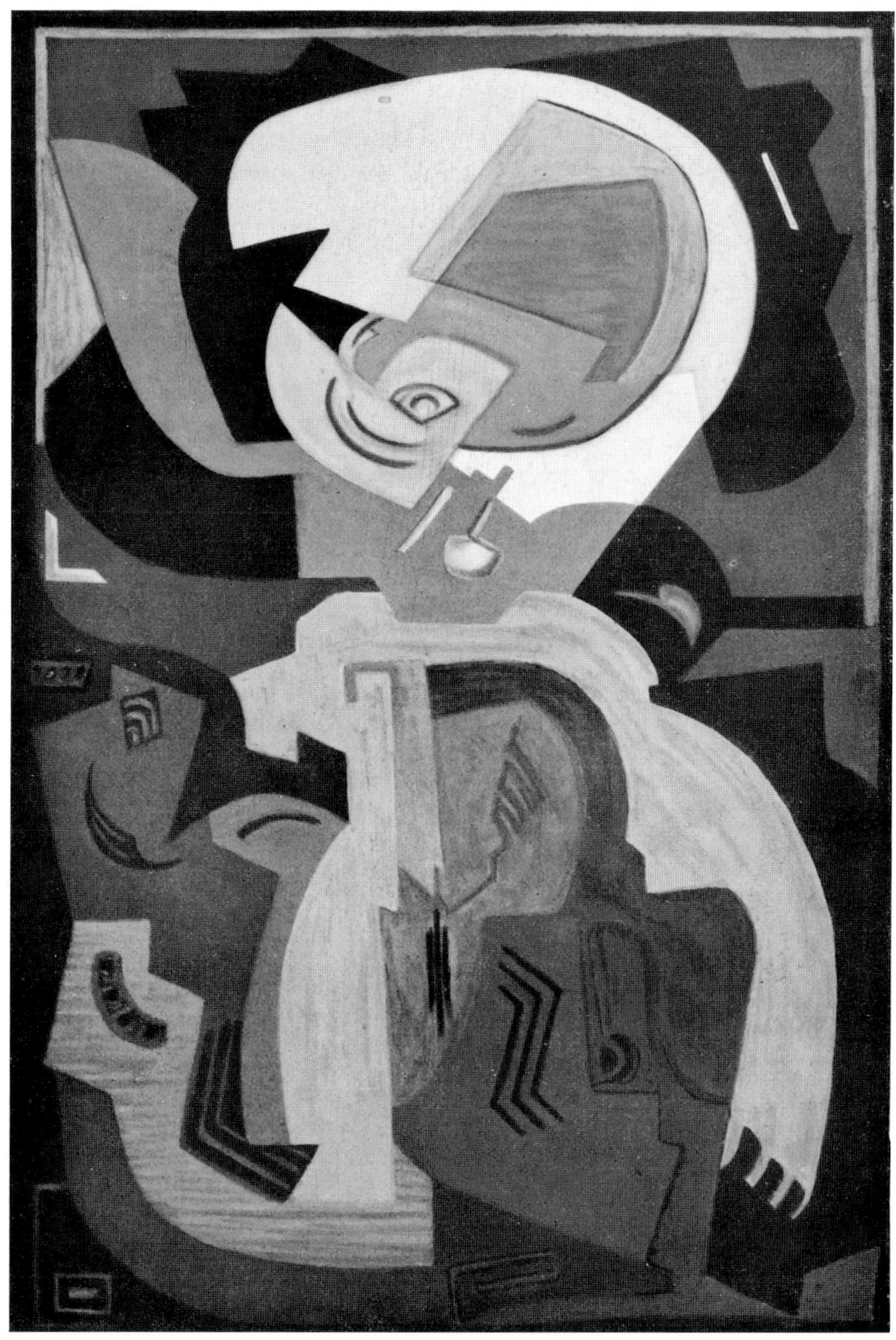

Fig. 46 Y. POSNANSKY COMPOSITION IN TWO BASIC FORMS. 1925

Third stage of Cubism. The same as in the previous example.

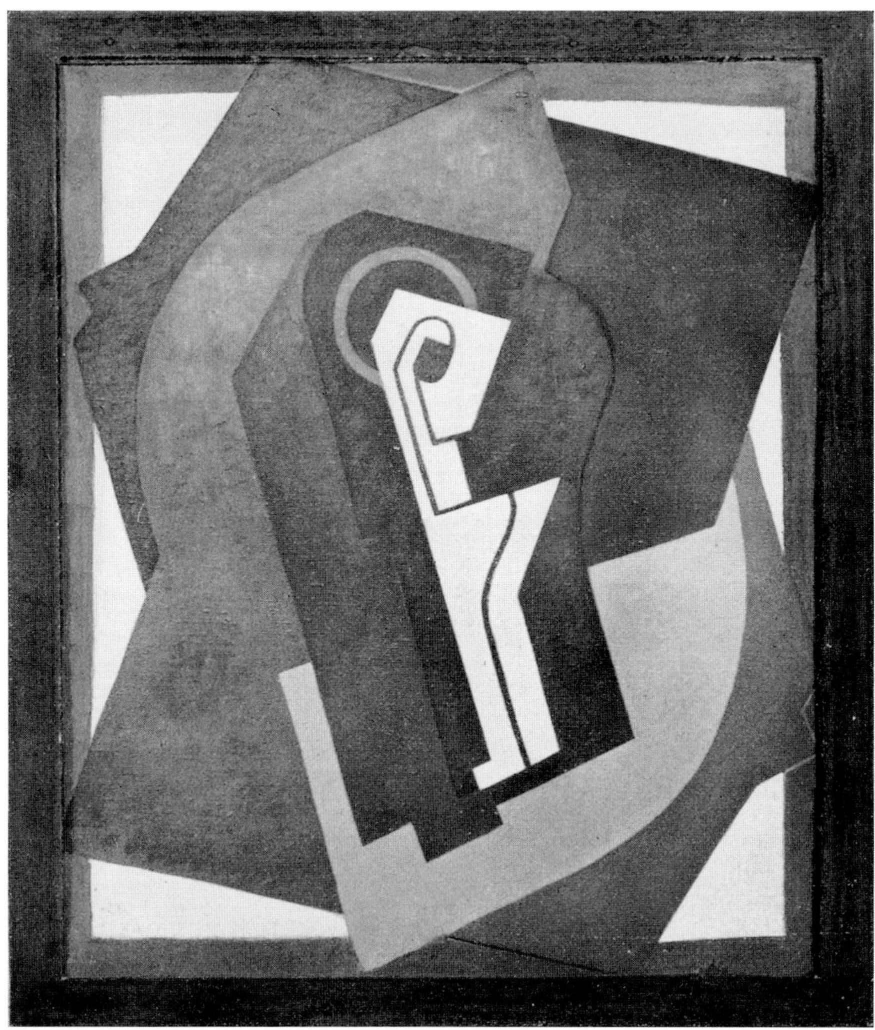

Fig. 47 ROBERT POUYAUD PAINTING. 1926

Third stage of Cubism. Organism of a rhythmic design based on the displacement and rotation of the surface.

II.

CUBISM
A NEW AWARENESS OF FORM
Attempt at a Generalization

ABRIDGED WITH THE AGREEMENT OF
THE AUTHOR BY EULEIN GROHMANN

The texts in the narrow columns are excerpts; the dots
(●) indicate places where the original text was shortened.

I.

Cubism is the reaction to a process which in the nature of the human race takes place everywhere; the transformation in painting is governed by the same causes as all the facts in the present crisis.

The present crisis is formal in nature and is the result of flawed design. Development is the artistic phenomenon in its various forms of intensity. Each process is a function of form. The human organism in isolation or as a whole is simply the vigor of the form. Malleability is the exclusive tendency of the entity to be realized in space. This law is the precondition for what we call life. Space is only there as a result of the relentless impact of this law.

It is a fundamental error that we did not clearly recognize this artistic fact (fait plastique); that we only discerned it at a particular point of its realization and failed to notice the earlier stages in which it was effective; this has resulted in a failure to recognize the universal harmony and consequently a contradiction in the way we understand its different values. ●

We should like to choose an example that demonstrates a unity of formal elements with various parameters (coefficient) whose interaction in no way disrupts the biological equilibrium. The correlation here lies in a continuous, uninterrupted development. This example is the structure of geometry. Geometry is based on a mere intellectual invention and abstraction: the point. When the point moves it becomes a line, the first reality: and when the latter moves in any direction, it creates another reality, the plane: finally the plane creates the body, a new reality, simply by virtue of the fact that it moves in the same way and thus conquers space by changing its position.

6*

Point, line, plane, body: this is the regular and coordinated structure of spatial reality, in other words, the theoretical and complete sequence of the artistic facts of life. And so the same term, "artistic fact," is applied to each of the terms in this series, in spite of the differences within the context of life which can be expressed through a parameter corresponding to the relevant degree of development.

Consequently, under no circumstances can we define this gradual formal structure as anything but geometric, nor may we understand a single phe‑ nomenon of this or that parameter as an artistic fact. ●

Each formal fact, from the point to the body, has a clearly delineated nature which determines it and beyond which it cannot go without surrendering itself. Thus the point does indeed become a line if it adopts a direction or an extension: the abstract becomes concrete; through its self‑destruction the point enables the formation of the line. If we observe this process through each stage of the conquest of space, we shall discover that the line ceases to be so that it can become the plane, and that the plane gives up its very nature in order to be resurrected in the new form of the body; the line, the first real appearance within the space, has advanced to the two dimensions of the plane, and this in turn has then advanced into the three‑dimensionality of the body. This results in a continuous direct development and perfect equilibrium, 0, 1, 2, 3.

This is how life in space looks when expressed in geometric terms; these are its different aspects as they are governed by the dimensions. The law to which the fact of creation is subject is thus expressly determined by directions and displacement, because we have not submitted ourselves sufficiently to the force of this law, which cannot simply be surrendered to human caprice. ●

The origin of the crisis and the reason for its momentous nature lie in the fact that we have failed to recognize the biological necessity of a renewal of the forms which have been acquired. We shall examine it from various sides in order to emphasize the tremendous importance of this fact in art and to show how unwise it is not to take it into consideration.

Point, line, plane and body are theoretical points of reference; all designs start out with them, but in daily life they do not exist in this pure form: They aim for it, approach it, are qualified by one element or another, are blurred, dark, visible, tangible, transitory, stable, reflect all forms of intuition and all dissimilarities.

If we abandon the purely geometric basis, we can observe the same compositional process in a purely human field, where there is sufficient freedom for the lively creative process to achieve the highest degree of perfection of spatial awareness. Thus in this field the different forms of expression of the so-called fine arts regain the significance which they had almost entirely lost: dance, music, poetry, painting, sculpture, and architecture.

●

The postulate of the abstract point for the structure of geometry and the postulate of the zero for the structure of arithmetic are fundamentally no different from the postulate of a divine will for the structure of the world. In the same way, mankind's will to create is a postulate for all the manifestations of human life.

We can now complete what we have said about the fact of development. Each procedure is a formal function. We know that the formal function belongs in the realm of geometry and that this process can only take place when on the other hand the wish for realization is evoked in another entity, in figures, in arithmetic. Thus it becomes clear that to create means to secure in time the energetic which runs unceasingly; to transform arithmetic into the geometric. This is where the entire secret of creativity lies, and we find it again constantly and everywhere. ●
Let us return to the realm of fine arts, where creative production is represented under the responsibility of people and under the most favorable conditions, where it seems to be most absolute. How can we recognize here the extent of the spatial? How can the number be understood?
Always according to the law of direction and change in position. The individual is at the same time the will of the number and the faculty of geometry. To a certain extent, therefore, the equivalent of the point. Direction and change in position become real through the simple fact of its movement. Dance is this first compositional proclamation of human order. It has the

reality of the line, is simultaneously both trendsetting and regulative. The human being realizes itself physically in that it arises once again in space and through itself under its own control. Now we recognize the significance of this process, and we realize why it is sacred in the origin of religious prac‑ tices. ●

To this day, dance remains a theoretical rhythmization of number in space through groups of people who have had a different development from us and who have preserved to the very last the ability to adapt their practices to the elementary and the essential; thus they veil their bodies in order to erase the memory of this, or they transform them by applying makeup, in order thereby to emphasize the creative process.

In connection with this wordless creative fact, a new form of expression of the line is soon revealed, if not a new formation of space: sound. When dance accelerates its movement, it creates onomatopoeia. This is formed like a nat‑ ural sound, more arithmetical than geometrical; it gives the impression of a small number of vibrations within a period of time, which therefore seem all the more exciting; it is a geometrical form, somewhat higher than that of dance, and perceptible through another sense, the ear. ● Dance and ono‑ matopoeia are the two forms of expression of the line. The starting point is the point, also known as the will of the subject, whereby the one so to speak satisfies the eye, and the other prompts the ear to hear.

These two creative processes give the sensory organ on which they work only a temporary and inadequate stimulus. The creative association that arises in that moment is dispelled again and the spatial falls back into formlessness and silence. ● In order to maintain the association for as long as possible, man will strive to create other artistic forms.

> It is on the basis of the linear foundations of dance that the formation of languages, writing and graphic drawing were developed.

In that, man continues to rely on the formal facts of the external surroundings, and having become aware of his existence in space, he will gradually recognize a formal state beyond that of the line, characterized by the shifting of the linear creative system within the space. This degree of creativity, which leads to the concept of the plane, thus links two directions which multiply the linear design with itself in a new sense, and fill out a new dimension in a completely new way by capturing a more perfect formal area. As a human arrangement, this second creative reality finds its dedication in painting. When thus through color or value, man expresses the return of the two-dimensional creative system on the originally preexisting extension of the surface progressively and according to recognized standards, he permits his eye to take possession, aware of a new state in the external surroundings. He no longer makes it his own in a temporary manner as in the case of dance, where the link is dissolved almost as soon as it has been created, nor does he do so in a descriptive way as in its fixation through writing, but through a lasting phenomenon full of reality, intensity, and life. Thus the space is captured in a new way through the fact that the desire for figures in turn has driven its geometric latency to realization.

The dominance of this desire for figures over the geometrical space will not stop here; it will continue to expand still further. The seizure of space will become more comprehensive; the space thus realized will open up new horizons; the law of direction and change of position will be applied across the entire surface, and human intellect will be able to encompass a higher form than the body. The formal facts which previously existed will find the confirmation of their explanation, the causes of their tangible dimensions, and sculpture, this rich formal phenomenon, will expand the ability of the eye, will surrender to it the selection of the location within the surroundings, from which the formal total effect can be assessed; under certain circumstances it will even satisfy the sense of touch. Thus, step by step, man has once again traveled along the path of his original biological evolution. Starting from his particular predisposition, he has restarted the arbitrary mechanism of creation within space. He has subjected his own state to the general laws that have determined him. ●

Every system of dimensions that corresponds to a diverse formal state nonetheless remains of the same kind as that from which it originates as well as that which is derived from it. That which is irreconcilable with the individualization acquires meaning once more in the universality of progress; the diverse views of the same individualization acquire their raison d'être through the shared aim which leads to their development. Dance, painting, and sculpture become linked together like the figures one, two, three; each limb is a perfect individualization in itself, and yet in unity with what goes before it and what will follow on. Onomatopoeia, word, music, writing — different forms of expression of the dimension of dance — subject themselves to the same goal within the development of form.

●

What is the consequence for man now that the directions of space are recognizable and realizable? To draw conclusions from them regarding the order of natural creation, that is to say to combine the three isolated design rules in their particular extent; to position oneself in the center of the space which allows then to come fully into the picture; and, in brief, to serve as fulcrum for all forms which these arrangements make accessible to the senses.

In order to arrive at this result, there is only one possible way: one will have to reach the highest stage of developmental progress, which has resulted from the destruction of what was subordinated to it. Since the result of two plus one equals three, and since it incorporates both, we shall only need to open three in order to find two plus one. Man has studied the body and has indeed found plane and line again; He has placed himself in the center voluntarily and responsibly. He has discovered that architecture ● is never determined by the individual scale, but always according to the collective one, according to the scale of creation in its absolute unity. Creation has moved in the direction of permanent improvement, whose peculiarity consists of an inversion, related to the significance of the two related factors, arithmetical time and geometrical space. Dance and music are in essence arithmetical; the minor geometrical vibrations of number and duration are ruled by time. Sculpture and architecture, on the other hand, are largely geometrical; to force together during the same period of time a much larger number of vibrations which the senses perceive as being short. In reality they have not changed the

immovable sizes of the geometric space; what changes is that what brings
them together or forces them apart, in other words movable time, distributes
their dimensions differently, according to the degree of the design. The sacred
movement of the beginning, dance, culminates in a sacred formal composi‹
tion, architecture, whose nature consists of the maintenance of a formal
association which, high above the individual subdivision, thereby evokes in
particular an impression of endless duration, in other words of eternity.

II.

Does the reader now begin to understand how important this formal fact is,
which during the different periods of its growth has surrounded the human
race with a secret that corresponds to the magnitude of his longing, his
delight at seeing it take shape, his disappointment at experiencing the disso‹
lution of the context?
The meaning of what we understand under the name of "artwork" becomes
clear; it regains validity in its original values which had been degraded
through the exclusive adaptation to the space, so that the facts of the form
which fulfill it were ultimately only adjusted to the restricted vicinity of the
sensory world. This misunderstood adaptation, which currently shows itself
in the fact that each individual endeavors to demonstrate the appearance
of the external forms as they appear to him at his particular position in
the space, has made us forget the true creative function. The result was a
kind of renunciation in favor of the constantly expanding conquest of
space, a renunciation which also took possession of the loftier facts which
because of their significance should really have offered protection from the
lapses of the individual. They too are caught up in the complicated network
of points of view that are never unambiguous because they continuously
change reality; nothing justifies them more finally in their claims to influence
the whole, because they are unable to understand it in its fundamental arith‹
metical truth.

Dance and music are purely formal facts, with the aim of giving; word and writing are related, with the aim of usefulness. Poetry has sometimes achieved the height of the gift. The poetry of today, like painting, suffers from the conflict between fine art and applied art, and is subject to the dictates of individual opinion.

The conflict between a creative beginning and the effect it produces, which appears as the starting point, is expedited and illustrated by painting. It expedites it inasmuch as it represents the new formal state which it was called upon to achieve and which results from the transition from the linear state to that of the plane, where the number of directions and the purpose of the shifts seem changed; it illustrates it inasmuch as it can only express an externally descriptive view by virtue of its characteristic of communicating as a whole with the senses all at once. So what really only needs to be hinted at in poetry suggests itself unambiguously in painting. The monotonous but active series of elements, arranged in the form of narrative verse, will no longer be comprehensible as soon as this narrative is suddenly reproduced through the nature of the flat surface.

Thus, even more than poetry, painting contributes to the distorting burden of the external illusion that serves as a support, which it has borrowed from the word and from language. ● It has been content to start with the word, with its meaning, and it has done nothing except to illustrate it. ● In this way, the progress of the composition has been inhibited, the law of direction and displacement were not observed, dimensions were distorted; measure and rhythm, which united the distinctions of the surroundings, considered them to be superfluous, and the individual narrated personal stories from his own particular point of view, often fascinating, but without a connection to the compositional aims which naturally strove to expand further into the space. ●

The highest level of composition is dominated by the dimensions of the body. It is here that the formal views of the exterior arise. In order to describe and interpret one's appearance as precisely as possible with the help of painting, you only need to pursue further in the plane the impression of the face which one gained in the surroundings. The achievement of this goal served the relativity of the perspective. Regardless of how interesting it may be for the understanding of an organic process, perspective has no compositional

credibility. It even destroys the form; it overturns the true relationships of the facts of the composition; it distorts the directions, suppresses measure and rhythm, and favors arbitrariness and lack of clarity. ●
We have lost the appreciation of the gradation of color (valeurs). With the help of perspective, we tried to explain theoretically the mechanism of the impression of a body in optical terms. We thought that this schematic demonstration of the physical was sufficient to realize a compositional fact on a flat surface. We successfully tricked the eye, but we did not reckon with the incorruptibility of the intellect; the intellect could not allow even for a moment such an obvious distortion, such an attack on compositional truth. ●
The same heresy can be seen in a different guise in sculpture, the next-highest stage on the compositional ladder. Thanks to the resilience of its materials, through which it maintains the geometric association for as long as possible, the impression is aroused that the sculpture is able to maintain a certain compositional reality, regardless of the intentions of the individual.
But these intentions have a characteristic in common, namely that as soon as they merge with the material to be worked, they deprive it of a part of its compositional existence; each blow on the stone reduces its duration. To the extent that as soon as the imitative idea is conveyed to the formal carrier, this will have ceased to live, will be extinguished, and its place will be taken by a list of external realities, more or less transformed by the unusual point of view that the sculptor has chosen. Basically, the compositional state of the body, determined by its three directions, has nothing to do with perspective. In that the perspective realizes the material in question in its absolute volume beyond its visible and tangible details, it subjects the sculpture to the same conditions, according to which it adapts the external facts to the eye of the viewer. ●
Architecture, too, will have to adapt to the modification of the surroundings in such a system of homogeneity, ● will become descriptive, anecdotal, and useless. It will recognize its purpose only in the cold and lifeless copy of the compositional facts of architecture, which it perceives in the surrounding space. ●
Thus, in our present development, ● everything has followed the same renunciation, and if man has been able to deceive himself for such a long time, then on the other hand he will not be able to mislead the pressure of the forces which prove that even without him they will continue to be eternally

effective. This pressure has increased today to such an extent that the resistance of the clutch of morality is no longer sufficient; it breaks through and kindles the unrest which it feels to a new reality.

> The moral decline associated with the dominance of the individual expresses itself not only in art, but also in all circumstances of human life. The apprehension of space no longer takes place organically or compositionally or logically, but out of consideration of usefulness, out of material desire for domination. Examples: errors of engineering, war, industrial and economic crises, politics, science, progress without the supervision of moral conscience, hopeless experiments, emerging from the falsification of facts. Just as perspective deceives the eye, so too does the word deceive the intellect. Cures for these crises lie in a new insight into the interior laws of life, in a new collective conscience.

II.

Where can we already recognize the new conscience that is forming? We return to the field of art, whose aberrations are well known, and examine whether certain forms of expression today are not simply surprising because we assess them on the basis of these aberrations, which are considered as the yardstick.

> In poetry, the Romantics made the first attempt to return to a creative form. The Symbolists continued their work.

The unrest could be seen most clearly in the field of painting, with the most marked effect on the lethargy of the whole and its decrepit traditions. It was in painting that the first irresistible attack on the basis of the system became tangible. With Cubism it was not just that a word was coined — not just an empty term — but a series of circumstances. ●
It is not unimportant to direct our attention to the point that can most easily cause misunderstandings: the contradictory attitude adopted at a certain

92

time by men who at the beginning of a movement represent some of the greatest talents in the service of the new idea. The frequently practiced habit of vastly overestimating one's individual responsibility results in the way one identifies the truth of the idea with the realization through the individ⸗ual who communicates the idea. Eventually, one finds oneself confusing the fate of the idea with the demise of those whom it made famous for a certain period of time. ●

The influence of an individual results from the fact that at a given time he may succeed best in expressing what is happening in the latent state of a group to which he belongs. If what he represents had happened earlier or later, this incorporation in the whole would have been negligible or without direct effect. This explains the fate of the precursors and the latecomers. They do not yet have — or no longer have — the means to make themselves heard. The fact that the influence of individuals can spread derives from the fact that they appeared at a favorable time. When their influence declines it is because it no longer falls on fertile ground. ● The fact that an individual at a given time has given an idea a definite form, and that it seems at a different one that everything is retracted or contradicted, by no means implies that the idea has disappeared. Under no circumstances should we confuse the end of a form with the end of an idea. To be precise, we should consequently not simply pursue an idea, as it was epitomized by an individual during a specif⸗ic period, and then come to premature conclusions about the signs of its particular degeneration. I have often pointed out this error, without belittling the significance of the individual case in the reconstruction of the collective conscience; I have said that, in order to gain a clear picture of this Cubism, which since its emergence has changed like a living and growing organism, we should not consider the current opinion of one of the path⸗breaking artists but rather the continued existence of an attitude which represented the common link at the beginning, which was proclaimed in thousands of state⸗ments, in extravagant creations of the younger and therefore unknown rep⸗resentatives. It is here that we must seek the continuation of the idea; because an idea is like life; it does not disappear because an individual is dead; it is somewhere and is always in a new supporter.

After we have said this, we can now understand the deep significance of the successive stages of Cubism. The roots of this so⸗called dispute in painting lie a long way back, in the soil of Romanticism. The Impressionists gave an undeniable stimulus for revolution. They were closer to us and independent of Cézanne. For reasons that are easy to understand, no one wanted to know anything about his constant efforts to create a world whose laws first had to be discovered in their entirety and which was revealed in an indirect attack on the nature of form. The rigid academic indifference was opposed by a lively interest which, depending on the attitude of the artist, began to play with the changeable views of the same form. Perspective lost something of its rigor by spanning these changeable points of view; sensory elements were distributed, especially by means of color, that transitory and seductive element, well suited to make one forget the multiplicity of the views. Because basically, it was the views of the surroundings that were confounded; the sense of their form was transformed. The Academy defended certain coherent mea-surements which were admittedly true under certain conditions, but which were no longer in keeping with the times. On the other side of the barricade, artists expressed their doubts in these measurements in a disrespectful re-structuring of these outdated forms; but they went no further. Even so, they admired Cézanne, this intellectual artist, who unceasingly took up composi-tional problems, who arrived at a clear if not a practically realized affirmation. He committed himself to a form of painting, free of verbal description, of the previous reproach which was justified only by the mechanism of the relation-ships between the surfaces, recorded in the world of the picture surface. Cézanne's last paintings are the conclusions of his existence as an explorer. We recognize in the various stages of this development the hesitant attempts and the partial fulfilment. Cézanne, who was under the influence of his times, was always inhibited by the external image or the objective memory of the museum. It prevented him from drawing up precepts when he digressed from the empirical. It was the task of Cubism to continue the liberating work of Cézanne in the method of making Romantic intuition into a thing of logical conscience. ●

The appearance of paintings whose apparent cause was the wish to realize volume, the cube, rightly gave rise to the term "Cubism." In fact this expres-sion arose in the face of the passionate representation of volume, which transformed the academic form four-sidedly, without abandoning it. Seen less superficially, here we have an encounter between the constructive princi-ple of space and the description of a fact within this space; the principle evidently won the upper hand, because its purist and most rigorous visualization was stronger than the flexible views which it assumed in the random surroundings. This was the f i r s t s t a g e of the methodical reassessment: this analysis of the surroundings, ascribed to the principle of its strongest expres=siveness for the senses. The descriptive discovered its common goal; it was compressed into a finitely controllable system of dimensions. But soon the volume revealed its ability to destroy the surroundings, into which people were trying to anchor it by force. An artifice displaced the simple description under a different point of view, that of a schematized phenomenon which arose under new conditions into a new environment controlled by specific dimensions that were different from those used by artists. The episodic de=scription gave way to the description of a mechanical phenomenon; like the previous one, this failed to result in a formal solution. Here, too, volume demonstrated its vigor, because its law in the space, realized by means of a perfect theoretical form, nonetheless had no impact on the dominance of the perspectival unity which the Academy loved so greatly. It even temporarily acquired the appearance as if this law was to testify on behalf of Academicism, because it stood in opposition to the independent artists who were working on the dissolution of the rigid form. It restored the descriptive form, in that it tended to emphasize too strongly its inner principle. However, since that was only a temporary state, we can see today that in reality this period was an overhead line from the laws of the Renaissance to those of a new state of mind that did not yet know its own laws. Volume appeared to be destructive, ultimately because this law, having come to a standstill in a form seen only from one angle, no longer corresponded to the multiplicity of appearances which the environment has for the man of today; this observation was already hinted at in the paintings of the artists who attached more importance to color than form. The attempt at compensation through the description of the successive states of a process is not satisfied with a single viewpoint that has been determined once and for all; the terms of statics and dynamics were apparently not unaware of the facts of painting. This was the s e c o n d s t a g e of Cubist development.

So volume ceased to rule supreme over paintings; the various views that were selected which best characterized them as objects used as a rebuke were de=picted on the same plane, side by side, according to their temperament and their properties, and thus offered the viewer the cinematographic recital of an isolated fact or a process. ● The compositions of this period are explanatory.

They start out from a multiplicity of ways of looking at the same object or juxtaposing a large number of different objects as a uniform whole. This attempt shows clearly a new aspect of the compositional problem; the mind grapples with the contradiction between the demands and the means of satisfying them; caught in the closed dimensions of the space, it senses the significance of the time factor and its flexibility in the interlinking of facts. This cinematographic element in the compositions demonstrates that the artists did not avoid the difficulties, as many people did, by dissolving the form of the painting through the appeal of the colored nuances; they were clearly still clumsy, but they looked the alarming secret of form straight in the eye. Through this new description of the external surroundings they at= tempted to realize a formal fact in which several times were shown together within the same space, or several spaces within the same time. This occurred in the years 1911 and 1912. At that time, it was hardly possible to give an account of the value of such an attempt which was made by both poets and writers in a parallel development.•) ●

The impossibility of depicting a real unity with these realistic fragments, brought rationally closer to each other, but kept apart from each other by a sensuous impossibility, resulted in the fact that Cubism attempted with other means to satisfy this need for balance. Artists had recognized either rationally or emotionally that what was preventing this unity was in fact the nature of the materials that they were using; the nature of painting was offering resistance. A descriptive painting arranged according to a single perspectival point of view justified itself; its rigidity was not obvious; while the painting dependent upon multiple perspectival points of view could no longer justify itself. ● Naturally, the Cubist painters therefore undertook to investigate precisely this nature of painting, obsessed with the idea of truth and so filled with an urge for knowledge that they refused to pursue a trail for even a moment longer as soon as they noticed that it led to a dead end — and then these painters were accused of having got lost within a system.

•) Here we should like to recall the names of artists like Barzun, Marinetti, Jules Romains, N. Beauduin, Divoire, Apollinaire, Voirol, Cendrars, and others, the only ones who — depending on their talents — provided evidence of a state of mind that was fundamentally different from the officially prevailing one; with more or less success, they started admittedly not to find new means, but at least those which had lain idle through centuries of neglect.

Among the materials available in painting for the realization of formal facts was the first, and the least controversial one: the surface of the canvas or the wall. ● And people wanted to incorporate the multiplicity of points of view into the nature of this surface, which really stood in contradiction to that bold project. The nature of this surface could not be reconciled with this multiplicity of time or space, because the surface presented itself as a whole in a manner which appeared absolute to the senses. The senses apprehended it simultaneously in all its aspects. So the descriptive did not correspond to the nature of this surface. ● A surface is expanse, and if the expanse is to be accessible to the sense to which it appeals, the face, then rationally it cannot encompass the three characteristics of logical time, past, present and future, as the descriptive word or even volume can do. It is a question of other worlds, as a consequence of which the conditions change. The descriptive explained itself in the succession, and similarly the multifaceted view of volume: so it contradicted the nature of the surface, when the descriptive spread itself out across it, either in the sense of classical convention and perspectival unity, or in the new way of reproducing the points of view and hence the images. Seen as a means of creating an illusion of an external fact for the eye, perspective lost its justification because this descriptive fact jeopardized the life of the surface in its compositional reality. What Monge had demanded of the artists really happened. The father of descriptive perspective had often expressed regret that artists did not record more frequently the knowledge regarding the phenomenon of perspective that they had acquired during the course of their work. But eventually the artists went even further than his wishes: they totally rejected this perspective with its mechanism for distortion. ● The surface appeared to be subjected to a single time but nonetheless obliged to satisfy the senses through an impression of the spatial. The different times of each point of spatial expansion across the surface should be dissolved in a perfect composition, in which all parts were arranged side by side, in other words: the different views of the space across the surface should be realized in the unity of the rhythm. This is the characteristic of the third stage of Cubism. It was without doubt the most important with a view to the work that was to be accomplished. The two first stages had allowed the individual temperament a considerable degree of freedom to express itself empirically. ● So far, there were no principles that were sufficiently persuasive that the works could be measured against them.

They were times in which the responsibility for the work lay far more in the talent than in the deeper wisdom that only comes from mastery. The third stage, on the other hand, was the one in which the resistance was put to the test. Now intuitive observations were no longer sufficient; it was necessary for them to become stabilized in people's awareness. Order was born.

The effect of this order was such that the Cubists who had hitherto resisted could now declare without hesitation that their painting was total reality, before they had any idea of the objects that it was to contain. It was a momentous affirmation; it positioned the ability to compose outside every invocation of a familiar form, because this appeared subsequently for reasons that were of no interest to this compositional reality. At the same time, it contained the admission that it no longer needed the mediation of the details of an external space for the arousal to take place. This arousal, which inexplicably somehow led the conscious construction, was determined at the same time by the eruption of the inner wish as well as through the multiplic= ity of external views which resounded in the sensuous receptive organs. As a result of the knowledge he had acquired, the artist was to give this arousal a form for his specific surroundings without demanding of those viewing it that they should identify with his opinion and his sensibility. The viewer finds himself facing a universal truth, whose effect he consequent= ly cannot escape. If he is sensitive, he will feel its entire poetry in the nature that surrounds him, a poetry which emanates from the mysterious drift of the ephemeral. He discovers it in the same way as in nature, which, without tiring the senses, is permitted to repeat the same law and yet which never uses the same form twice. The compositional facts of the order "Surface" are similarly individualized, as the facts in space all are too; each one always has the opportunity of renewing itself in a minor way, and yet it remains subject to the eternal, unchangeable laws.

●

So Cubism has fundamentally overturned the traditional concept of painting, ● the old descriptive concept which was supported by the analytical per= spective. It reintroduces a liberated mentality in a new order with a biolog= ical mechanism which adjusts to the undeniable fate of modern mankind. I say "reintroduces," because we cannot naively believe that this order and the mental state which supports it have appeared for the first time. ● The order is not new; only the mechanical means of expressing it can be renewed. That is not much, but it is sufficient to continue life. ●

The order which Cubism reinstates is a natural order in the sense that it has not established itself on rational achievements. ● Cubism is a transfor‑ mation of thought, of a state of mind, which, the clearer it became in itself, the clearer was the awareness with which it realized its methods and its means.

Two constants have returned beyond the applied forms; they are both funda‑ mental requirements for this fact of composition. ● These constants are rhythm and expansion. Rhythm is the flowing, agile, numerical, arithmetical quantity, expansion the constant, static, pictorial, geometrical one. So now it was only necessary to set this dynamic rhythm in motion within the matter of the static expansion. In the hands of the artist and under the control of his eyes, the static expansion was the surface of the canvas. The rhythm was the beating of his own heart, evoked by his mind. His intellectual ability, which alone is capable and apart from which there is nothing, had the task of regulating these two selected elements. ● And so, at the end, a perfect organism would be created, balanced, in proportion, rhythmic, which alone is based in the harmonious juxtaposition of his organs, in the complete interpenetration of quality and quantity. Finally, from now on it would be possible, for everyone who wanted to, to enjoy these aspects of life; they have their own static form, which comes to life through the dynamic movement, a form which arouses the senses, a movement which arouses the spirit. ●

Since the surface had to be respected by virtue of its formal life, the technique became easier. No longer bound to the imitative description, it once more became true and good, simple and direct. The compositional fact could be realized again, before the artist thought of the objects that appeared at ran‑ dom: mastery took the place of improvisation. I use the word in the former sense of craftsmanship, as a position in the hierarchy of values and not in the coarse and conceited sense that we give it today. Mastery guaranteed the freedom of craftsmanship. ●

So the colors were applied to the surface, in the manner of a craftsman who pays attention to the particular nature of the surface. They developed with the surface and their shades determined the value of the rhythmic structuring in their original expansion. Color and shade no longer needed to exercise a

sentimental appeal; they were to underline, to confirm to the senses and the intellect the continuing development of a formal fact which was of the same kind as any natural structure. 
A work created in this way enjoys the advantages of natural creations. They relate nothing; they say nothing; they imitate nothing; it is sufficient for them to be there, subjected to the surroundings and their changes. They adapt their own, and the light of the surroundings enables them to appear in their vitality, particularly as their substance is dependent on this light. But the work created by man can be even more illuminating and its purity even more approximate than the natural creations. It must make their dimensions, relationships, proportions tangible. ●
All this lies far from the mental state of our time, which is in the process of dissolution; the language that we speak will only be heard by those who have already traveled part of the journey, who even if they do not belong to Tomorrow, are nevertheless no longer willing to serve Today.

●

I have tried to execute the particular case of painting in a general manner, because from here all manifestations of human activity and those which are independent of man hurl themselves at the conquest of space as if it were all the determination of a single will. Have I succeeded in providing an explanation of the term "Cubism" not only for the experts but especially for the much larger numbers of those who are called upon to recognize the nature of Cubism, by stressing its true meaning, which extends far beyond the material fact of the work itself? I should like to hope so all the more because I am convinced of the earnestness of the present conflict; it will manifest itself in inextricable external emotions until those who know its more profound origin join together, in order to help the new thought achieve real power and support it through the number of its supporters. Because there is no viable form in space without a creative intellectual power which precedes it; a new order can establish itself on a rejuvenated mental state which has reestablished contact with the source, adapted to the needs of the present day, which thus expands the intellectual progress of mankind by a term.
Each one of us still clings to the era that is coming to an end. ● Human nature consists of this dualism. We have not yet sufficiently determined its being.

100

Man is simultaneously both a free agent and a social being. To what extent does he take part in the community? When does he belong to himself? To find the answer to these questions means finding the solution in its true foundations, it means determining the common denominator of all today's contradictions. ●

After all that, this representation of Cubism can be of use. People will doubtless understand what is really vital behind this expression, and those who have often stood in front of paintings of this kind without fathoming their meaning will now know that a complete thought was composed there, a thought which sought a human basis in the widest sense, in order to express itself simply and directly. Since the appearance of Cubism, which now lies a long time ago, many manifestations bearing the suffix "ism" have apparently taken its place; but in reality they were only more or less differentiated forms of expression of the same idea, if we consider not so much the word as the intellectual intention. The painters of 1910 demonstrated clearly that they were not slaves of a single word. Not only that they by no means invented the term that people forced upon them; they were also completely independent of this term, and the more they expressed their intentions through their works, the more they rejected it. Their most vigorous opponents often considered it to be the best policy to spread throughout public opinion the fact that Cubism was moribund, that it was already dead, or even buried; they were right, because from it painting developed as a simple craft like any other. Its roots went back to the simplest house painter and it grew to mastery, this exemplary application of a technique of the highest order and the greatest perfection.

1925

BAUHAUSBÜCHER

SCHRIFTLEITUNG: WALTER GROPIUS
L. MOHOLY-NAGY

			Abbildungen	steif brosch.	i. Leinen geb.
1	Walter Gropius,	INTERNATIONALE ARCHITEKTUR. Zweite Auflage. Auswahl der besten neuzeitlichen Architekturwerke.	96	Mk. 5	Mk. 7
2	Paul Klee,	PÄDAGOGISCHES SKIZZEN-BUCH. Zweite Auflage. Aus seinem Unterricht am Bauhaus mit von ihm selbst gezeichneten Textillustrationen.	87	Mk. 6	Mk. 8
3	Ein Versuchshaus des Bauhauses.	Neue Wohnkultur; neue Techniken des Hausbaues.	61	vergriffen	
4	Die Bühne im Bauhaus.	Theoretisches und Praktisches aus einer modernen Theaterwerkstatt.	42 3 Farbtafeln	Mk. 5	Mk. 7
5	Piet Mondrian,	NEUE GESTALTUNG. Forderungen der neuen Gestaltung für alle Gebiete künstlerischen Schaffens.		vergriffen	
6	Theo van Doesburg,	GRUNDBEGRIFFE DER NEUEN GESTALTENDEN KUNST. Versuch einer neuen Ästhetik.	32	vergriffen	
7	Neue Arbeiten der Bauhauswerkstätten.	Praktische Beispiele neuzeitlicher Wohnungseinrichtung.	107 4 Farbtafeln	Mk. 6	Mk. 8
8	L. Moholy-Nagy,	MALEREI, FOTOGRAFIE, FILM. Zweite Auflage. Apologie der Fotografie, zugleich grundlegende Erkenntnis abstrakter und gegenständlicher Malerei.	100	Mk. 7	Mk. 9
9	Kandinsky,	PUNKT UND LINIE ZU FLÄCHE. Zweite Auflage. Beitrag zur Analyse der malerischen Elemente.	127 1 Vierfarben-Druck	Mk. 12	Mk. 15
10	J. J. P. Oud,	HOLLÄNDISCHE ARCHITEKTUR. Zusammenfassung theoretischer und praktischer Erkenntnis auf dem Gebiete der Architektur.	39	Mk. 6	Mk. 9
11	Kasimir Malewitsch,	DIE GEGENSTANDSLOSE WELT. Die Geschichte und Begründung des russischen Suprematismus.	92	Mk. 6	Mk. 8
12	Walter Gropius,	BAUHAUSNEUBAUTEN IN DESSAU. Der Bauhausneubau und die Meisterhäuser.	etwa 100	Mk. etwa 7	Mk. etwa 9
13	Albert Gleizes,	KUBISMUS. Die Geschichte des Kubismus.	47	Mk. etwa 6	Mk. etwa 8
14	L. Moholy-Nagy,	VON KUNST ZU LEBEN. Der Weg zum Erlebnis von Plastik und Architektur.	etwa 150	Mk. etwa 8	Mk. etwa 10

ALBERT LANGEN VERLAG
MÜNCHEN / HUBERTUSSTRASSE 27

bauhaus

zeitschrift des bauhauses für bau und gestaltung
verlag und geschäftsstelle: dessau, zerbsterstr. 16

die zeitschrift erscheint vierteljährlich
bezugspreis jährlich mk. 4.—
mitglieder des „kreis der freunde des bauhauses"
erhalten die zeitschrift kostenlos